MIX-
TAPE
POT-
LUCK

A dinner party for friends, their recipes, and the songs they inspire.

Questlove

With Ben Greenman
and Lauren Schaefer

Photography by
Marcus Maddox

**Abrams Image
New York**

A Cookbook

MIX-TAPE POT-LUCK

Planted about two decades ago, back in Philly, was the seed that grew into the tree that forced open the floodgates of creativity, both artistically and socially. That seed was the original Black Lily Jam sessions. Back then, we sensed—we knew—that the thing that would unite us, that would help us make music and conversation, would be food. We hired a chef (thank you, Chef Terry!), and he cooked, and that cooking banded us together: We cooked as a band. Food is the oldest form of communication and community, and this is an attempt to replicate and renew that energy.

Food is also family, so I want to offer thanks to the people who provided the food memories that I hold near and dear to this day: to Nana and the Saturday pancakes at her house, which were a major event (sometimes it was Aunt Barbra or Uncle Junie); to Aunt Laura, who hosted the post-church soul-food gatherings; to my cousin Joanne, who is pretty much the best chef I'll ever know in this lifetime; to Mom, making her version of my fave arroz con pollo (translation *roya ca poya*); to Donn, making Jiffy Pop while we watched *SNL* and then *Soul Train* at 1 A.M.; especially to Tariq and Richard for the surprise dishes they'd invent during our starving-artist days living in the UK. These memories live forever in my stomach, in my mind, in my heart. Thank you.

10   Foreword—*Martha Stewart*
14   Introduction
20   Guest List

Arrival Snacks

24   Fresh and Smoked Salmon Rillette
     with Sourdough Toast—*Éric Ripert*
26   Pimento Cheese Dip with
     Biscuit Crackers—*Carla Hall*
28   Studio Standard (Cocktail Spread)—*Tom Sachs*
34   Plantains Two Ways—*Fred Armisen*
36   Grape Focaccia—*Martha Stewart*
40   Guacamole—*Dustin Yellin*
42   Roasted Kale Chips—*Ardenia Brown*
44   Jalapeño Salmon Fish Skins with Blistered
     Shishito Peppers—*Ardenia Brown*

Start It Up: Small Plates

48   Chickpea and Spinach Tapas—*Padma Lakshmi*
50   Crab Rangoon—*Greg Baxtrom*
52   Perfect No-Roll Crab Roll—*Ignacio Mattos*
55   Poached Chicken Wraps—*Camille Becerra*
58   Sweet Potato Kimchi Pancake—*Nyesha Arrington*
60   New Orleans–Style BBQ Shrimp and
     Burrata Toast—*Kelly Fields*

BRING IT RIGHT ON OVER! SOUPS AND STEWS

66   Chocolate Chili—*Maya Rudolph*

68   Shep's Maui Onion and Ginger Soup—*Shep Gordon*

70   South Philly Seafood Stew—*Tariq Trotter*

72   Mexican Corn Chowder (There Is No
      Such Thing)—*Alex Stupak*

76   Mom's Chicken Curry—*Lilly Singh*

RIGHT THERE NEXT TO IT: SIDES AND SALADS

80   Bok Choy and Cucumber Salad—*Zooey Deschanel*

82   Peppers à la Famiglia Tomei—*Marisa Tomei*

84   Herbed Shrimp Salad with Fried Green
      Tomatoes and Romaine—*Edouardo Johnson*

88   Tomato Salad with Nectarines, Basil, and
      Bagna Cauda—*Flynn McGarry*

90   Tomato/Potato Salad—*Jessica Koslow*

VEG FRIENDS YOU WANNA IMPRESS

94   Easy Veggie Party Quiche (That Will
      Blow Everyone's Minds)—*Amy Poehler*

96   Open-Face Lemon Cornbread Mushroom Sliders
      with Maple Chipotle Aioli—*Haile Thomas*

99   Roasted Veggie Quinoa Bowl—*Kimbal Musk*

102   Spinach Pie—*Natalie Portman*

104   Whole Roasted Cauliflower with
      Two Sauces—*Jessica Seinfeld*

CARB JONEZ

108 Kale Walnut Pesto Pasta—*Ashley Graham*

110 Nastassia's Baked Pasta Frittata—*Mark Ladner*

114 Tuna Pasta à la Popowendy—*Humberto Leon*

116 Old Dirty Basmati Rice—*Tanya Holland*

122 Jollof Rice with Jerk Chicken and Marinated Gooseberries—*Kwame Onwuachi*

125 Coconut Jollof Rice—*Yvonne Orji*

MEAT EATERS

132 Air-Fried Chicken Burgers—*Jimmy Fallon*

134 Heidi's Million Dollar Chicken—*Carol Lim*

138 Thịt Kho Tàu (Vietnamese Braised Pork Belly)—*Kevin Tien*

141 Lamb Chops with Mint Salsa over Couscous—*Athena Calderone*

144 Spicy Sweet and Sour Chicken with Lemongrass—*Andrew Zimmern*

147 JJ's Sticky Ribs—*J. J. Johnson*

152 Country Captain Chicken—*Mashama Bailey*

154 Braised Osso Buco with Fennel Soffritto—*Missy Robbins*

156 Fried Rabbit—*Chris Fischer*

BITTERSWEET ENDING

164 Blueberry Crunch Cake—*Jessica Biel*

166 Fruit Salad with Cucumber and Mint—*Melody Ehsani*

168 Cinnamon Rolls with Honey Mead Icing—*Dominique Ansel*

171 Corny Shortcakes with Strawberries and Sour Whipped Cream—*Christina Tosi*

174 Tiramisu Tradizionale—*Joey Baldino*

RAISE A GLASS

178   Ginger Beer—*Thelma Golden*

180   Bourbon Raspberry Tea—*Gabrielle Union*

182   Kether's Favorite Cocktail:
            "Me and Mia" from Tramp Stamp Granny's
            Bar in LA—*Kether Donohue*

184   Red Skies at Night—*Dave Arnold*

AFTER THE AFTER PARTY: LATE NIGHT SNACKS

190   Grilled Bologna Sliders on Hawaiian
            Rolls—*Matty Matheson*

192   Eggs in Purgatory—*Stanley Tucci*

194   Mac and Cheese—*Q-Tip*

198   Tina's Cold Pizza—*Jarobi White*

200   "Heimy's Happiness" Fries with Kewpie Mayo,
            Caviar, and a Glass of Bubbles—*Eric Wareheim*

202   Afterword: If You Can't Cook,
            You Still Can Help

208   *Mixtape Potluck* Guest List-Inspired Playlist

212   Playlist Tips

216   Index

FOREWORD: MARTHA STEWART

I was thrilled when Ahmir Khalib Thompson—aka Questlove—asked me to write the foreword to his latest non-music venture, a cookbook titled *Mixtape Potluck*. Thrilled because the assignment was an opportunity to learn a little bit more about this apparently imposing musician who is always onstage leading the *Tonight Show* band when I do a skit on Jimmy Fallon. Thrilled because his interest in my food-related segments always intrigued me. Now, I can understand why he always stuck close during those segments, why he was so inquisitive—he is a foodie. And he is as truly involved with food as he is with music. He is eloquent about that interest, writing about food, caring about dishes, trying out recipes, and thinking about the effect that food, dishes, and recipes have on his friends and acquaintances.

For years, I was not a fan of potluck dinners. When I was growing up in the smallish town of Nutley, New Jersey, "potluck" connoted a buffet of random casseroles, most homemade, of varying goodness; big, somewhat ill-conceived salads; and Jell-O molds, box desserts, or bakery bought cakes. I always preferred making all the food myself, serving my guests my recipes and my creations, and leaving nothing to chance. But now that I have a show on VH1 with Questlove's buddy Snoop Dogg, aptly named *Martha and Snoop's Potluck Dinner Challenge*, of course I am interested in all things potluck, and especially in this new recipe book by Questlove.

I am curious about the types of recipes and music one would serve at a potluck designed by the inimitable Questlove. Of all the recipes he's been served on the *Tonight Show*, in restaurants, which would he choose to include in his collection of favorites? Which friends would he ask? How would he organize the dinner?

I was also curious how he would fit the potluck dinner into his larger set of activities. Questlove is omnipresent: He is in Puerto Rico one weekend DJing alongside a performance of *Hamilton*. The next week he might be at the *Time* 100 gala. And every night he's on TV with the Roots, providing music for the king of late night, Jimmy Fallon. Along the way, he eats, and pays attention to what he's eating, hobnobbing with chefs and cooks and cookbook authors. This book brings together not only a set of recipes from friends who have been invited to his dream potluck, but his unerring choices of what he calls "Song Prompts" for each recipe. When he asked Dominique Ansel to make a dessert, he had in his mind the Ohio Players' "Sweet Sticky Thing"; the recipe turned out to be an amazing one, for cinnamon rolls. For my prompt, of course, he gave out Snoop's "Life of Da Party." The recipe I contributed should stay a secret until you get there. Hint: It's not that far into the book.

So thank you, Questlove, for this inspired book on a theme that is having a resurgence thanks to you, me, and Snoop, and all those other home cooks who want to treat their families, friends, and loved ones to something special, something personal, something homemade and good. I guess all of us want to be invited to one of Questlove's potlucks. I'll bring something for any course you ask me to bring!

—Martha Stewart

What Is a Mixtape Potluck?

Is it an idea? An event? A piece of performance art? A magic show? Does it involve dozens of people assembling in the same place at the same time? Is it capable of producing various kinds of satisfaction for the body and the mind?

The answer to all the questions except the very first one is yes, and the answers to all the others are the answer to the very first one.

For years now, I have been throwing dinner parties. I call them food salons. I have any number of people over—not any number, but the number varies—and I invite chefs from the country's top restaurants to cook for them. The chefs make dishes that can be eaten partly standing up, because that's what happens: people take their food on plates and walk around, talking, laughing, and telling stories. For the guest list, I try to draw on all the different worlds that I'm lucky enough to be in: the music world, the TV world, the comedy world, the design world, the literary world, the technology world.

The food salons are a great place to meet people, to catch up with people, and to enjoy people's company. They are also a great place for casual epiphanies. I know, because about a year ago, I had one myself. I was standing in the middle of a food salon looking out across the crowd when it occurred to me that I should throw a different kind of party. Rather than invite chefs to cook, I should invite the guests to cook. Guests are always telling me that they have a super-special secret recipe some-where in their family, an amazing shrimp stew or vegetarian lasagna, and that they have to make it for me sometime. Okay, then. Why not make that sometime happen? Why not design an event where everyone makes that super-special secret recipe, all at once?

That's the Potluck part of this cookbook. Right behind it came the Mixtape part. It might not even have been behind it. It might have sprung into my mind at the same time, as part of that same epiphany. I decided that I would select a song to inspire each guest to cook. It wouldn't be a song specifically designed to direct them to cook a certain dish. (I didn't want to tell them what to do.) It wouldn't be a song that reflected the dish they ended up cooking. (How would I know what that would be?) It would be a song suggested to me by the people who were cooking, by what I knew of them and their creative lives. Fairly early on, I realized that not every contributor needed a prompt in the same way. Some people already had recipes in mind. Others wanted to play out their own creative string without outside direction. As a result, the songs and the dishes do not have a direct relationship. You can't put each song into a machine and then run around to the other side and collect the dish. Take them in the spirit they were given: as creative inspiration.

Also, it's important to clarify how the music in this book should be used. The songs next to each recipe are not songs that are part of my ideal dinner party playlist. Do not be confused by that. I did build an ultimate dinner party playlist. It's at the end of Chapter 10. That's what you'll hear if you come to my house for the next amazing potluck. The songs on each recipe in this book aren't for entertainment purposes in that sense. They're for your personal use. They're a way of introducing you to the contributors and to a song that helped me to think through their creative contribution. I hope that the songs—and the people—inspire you as well. Listen to them. Love them. Use them as you see fit.

As the idea of the *Mixtape Potluck* started to come together, I was clear about one thing, which is that I wouldn't be cooking. I, myself, am not really a cook. It's the one area of my life where I feel like a total impostor. I'm not saying I can't cook. I have enough creative experience in other areas (and enough of a sense of my own energies) that I probably would make it happen. But time does not permit. The only time I will cook is in a relationship, and mostly at the beginning, and when making popcorn (which is not really considered cooking).

This book was a pleasure to make. It is a pleasure to still be making it. But it is also a pleasure to use. *Mixtape Potluck* isn't just a document of the most awesome party I could have ever imagined. It's a cookbook, and a real one. Each recipe has been tested in a kitchen and eaten by analytically minded humans. Each recipe can in turn be whipped up in a kitchen by you, the reader, or anyone you decide to give this book to as a gift. The dishes are optimal for large groups, and for that matter for large loud groups who combine their eating with spirited discussions of ideas already done and ideas still to do. Put plates and dishes in the center of a big table. Point your guests to them. Watch as those guests go to town. My fondest hope is that you use this cookbook in both ways: to cook quietly for you and/or your immediate family and to put together Mixtape Potlucks of your own. And there is an interactive component. When you cook, pay attention to what music you're playing in the background. See if the music affects what you do. Also pay attention to what music comes to mind when you're eating. Sometimes, as I say, the fit will be perfect. Sometimes it will be perfectly imperfect and produce productive tension. When you're done cooking and eating and done paying attention to what happened during both of those stages, share the results. **#MixtapePotluck**. I want to hear about your matches and mismatches, your happy accidents and your train wrecks. Include photographs. If there's one thing this book has taught me, it's that creative acts are like musical notes. They sustain if you encourage them.

I wanted, above all, to promote the idea of food as a communal experience. Many art forms are, to some degree. When you listen to music, you can do it alone, but it's different—and, some would argue, more rewarding—to go to a show and sit among hundreds of other people who are hearing the same thing you are. You can stream a movie on your laptop, but it's different—better—to see it in a crowded theater. Food, at least the way I like to think about it, follows a similar principle. You can hire one of the world's great talents—whether it's a chef at a renowned restaurant or your grandma, who happens to make the best lasagna known to humankind—to make a meal just for you. You can cook for yourself. I know people at work who make five-course meals for themselves. I get a little sad when they're talking about it:

"This weekend I made a crab bake." It sounds delicious, but they live alone. If that's how you're doing it, maybe you're not getting the most out of it. The pleasure you feel, the sensations you experience, are amplified and reflected by the people around you. They are a force multiplier and also a kaleidoscope. For me, eating with a big group of friends and family is like playing a live show or seeing a movie in a theater. It's the ultimate experience.

Before I got started sending out music to all my guests, I realized that I had to pick a song for myself. I needed a practice run before the big show. I went through lots of songs about parties, eating, eating at parties, cooking, chefs, kitchens, utensils, tables, chairs, and chewing. The song that kept surfacing in my mind was Cab Calloway's "Everybody Eats When They Come to My House." It's a novelty song from 1948 in which Cab welcomes a number of people to his house, rhyming names with dishes until the whole thing becomes a surreal mix of guests and dishes. There are a number of stanzas, but the first one gives a pretty complete account of the way the thing works:

> *Have a banana, Hannah*
> *Try the salami, Tommy*
> *Get with the gravy, Davy*
> *Everybody eats when they come to my house.*

I picked that song for myself, and then I realized that I wasn't just picking it for myself. I was picking it for the whole potluck. Everybody eats when they come to my house. Truer words have never been sung.

—Questlove
November 1, 2018

GUEST LIST

ERIC RIPERT
CARLA HALL
TOM SACHS
FRED ARMISEN
MARTHA STEWART
DUSTIN YELLIN
ARDENIA BROWN
PADMA LAKSHMI
GREG BAXTROM
IGNACIO MATTOS
CAMILLE BECERRA
NYESHA ARRINGTON
KELLY FIELDS
MAYA RUDOLPH
SHEP GORDON
TARIQ TROTTER
ALEX STUPAK
LILLY SINGH
ZOOEY DESCHANEL
MARISA TOMEI

EDOUARDO JORDAN

FLYNN McGARRY

JESSICA KOSLOW

AMY POEHLER

HAILE THOMAS

KIMBAL MUSK

NATALIE PORTMAN

JESSICA SEINFELD

ASHLEY GRAHAM

MARK LADNER

HUMBERTO LEON

TANYA HOLLAND

KWAME ONWUACHI

YVONNE ORJI

JIMMY FALLON

CAROL LIM

KEVIN TIEN

ATHENA CALDERONE

ANDREW ZIMMERN

JJ JOHNSON

MASHAMA BAILEY

MISSY ROBBINS

CHRIS FISCHER

JESSICA BIEL

MELODY EHSANI

DOMINIQUE ANSEL

CHRISTINA TOSI

JOEY BALDINO

THELMA GOLDEN

GABRIELLE UNION

KETHER DONOHUE

DAVE ARNOLD

MATTY MATHESON

STANLEY TUCCI

Q-TIP

JAROBI WHITE

ERIC WAREHEIM

JANINA GAVANKAR

ARRIVAL

SNACKS

When I host a dinner party, those first moments are vital. It's never too early to make a first impression. Because of that, I always want to make sure to have something tasty for my guests to eat as soon as they walk through the door. I don't know about you, but people come to my house hungry and ready to jump into it right away. Music is already on the sound system—start with instrumentals so that the conversations can grow without competition—and snacks are already served. Whether you are bringing a snack to someone's home or pre-paring snacks for your own potluck, trust me, this first little bite will be one of the most appreciated. These snacks may go quickly, but you can replenish them for people who arrive a little later.

Fresh and Smoked Salmon Rillette with Sourdough Toast
Éric Ripert

Serves: 12 to 15
Prep time: 15 minutes, plus at least 30 minutes refrigeration
Cook time: 5 minutes

Chef Ripert is one of the nicest people I know, and the dish he made reflects that niceness. It's convivial and convenient, conducive to eating while you move around and talk to other people. It's like friendliness in food form. Serving note: It's perfect with pre-dinner champagne or cocktails.

- 1 (750-ml) bottle dry white wine
- 2 shallots, roughly chopped
- 2 teaspoons salt, plus more to taste
- 2 pounds (910 g) salmon fillets, fat trimmed, cut into 1-inch (2.5-cm) cubes
- 6 ounces (170 g) smoked salmon, cut into small dice
- ¼ cup (60 ml) fresh lemon juice
- 1 cup (215 g) mayonnaise
- Freshly ground black pepper
- 2 tablespoons thinly sliced fresh chives
- Toasted sourdough or a fresh baguette, sliced to your liking

Combine the wine, shallots, and 1 teaspoon of the salt in a large saucepan and bring to a boil over medium heat. Lower the heat so it is at a lively simmer and add the fresh salmon. Poach for 40 seconds. Drain in a sieve, discarding the poaching liquid. Place the salmon in a large bowl and refrigerate until cold, about 30 minutes.

Add the smoked salmon to the bowl with the poached salmon and use the side of a wooden spoon to gently break up the salmon pieces. Stir in the lemon juice, mayonnaise, the remaining 1 teaspoon salt, and pepper to taste. Add the chives, taste, and add more salt if needed. Cover and keep chilled until ready to serve.

Transfer the rillette to a serving bowl and serve with toasted bread slices.

Whenever I've been to Le Bernardin, where Éric is the chef, I've been amazed by the way that everything is arranged. I guess I mean that conversationally, but I also mean it musically. The restaurant combines elements of composition and improvisation, like classical music shading into jazz. There's also a giant painting of the ocean, which means that when I'm in that room I hear, inside my own head, Joshua Redman's cover of Led Zeppelin's "The Ocean." Redman does something tricky, taking a song of immense power and transforming it into something delicate. That's what Éric does, but using food instead of music. He harnesses and channels power, and the result is delicacy and wonder.

Pimento Cheese Dip with Biscuit Crackers

Carla Hall

Serves: 15 to 20
Prep time: 10 minutes,
plus at least 1 hour refrigeration
Cook time: 20 minutes

Carla's appetizer is, as it turns out, capable of feeding an entire family. It should come with a warning: Your Guests May Fill Up On This. Language note: *Pimiento* is a loanword, a Spanish word that we brought into English and used for our own purposes. Carla's dish is a loandish.

For the Crackers:
- 6 day-old biscuits, homemade or store-bought
- 4 tablespoons (56 g) butter, melted
- 1 teaspoon kosher salt
- ¼ teaspoon cayenne pepper

For the Pimento Cheese:
- 4 ounces (115 g) cream cheese, softened
- ½ cup (107 g) mayonnaise
- 2 cloves garlic, grated
- 1 teaspoon cayenne pepper
- 1 whole roasted red bell pepper from a jar, finely diced
- ½ teaspoon kosher salt
- 8 ounces (227 g) sharp Cheddar cheese, grated
- 8 ounces (227 g) Monterey Jack cheese, grated

To make the biscuit crackers: Preheat the oven to 400°F (205°C). Line two baking sheets with parchment and butter the parchment.

Cut the biscuits from top to bottom into ⅛-inch (3-mm) slices. Place the slices on the prepared baking sheet about ½ inch (12-mm) apart.

In a small bowl, mix together the salt and cayenne and evenly season the biscuits with the mixture.

Bake for 7 minutes, then flip and bake for an additional 7 minutes, or until golden brown. Transfer to a wire rack and let cool before serving.

To make the pimento cheese: While the biscuits are baking, combine the cream cheese, mayonnaise, garlic, cayenne, bell peppers, and salt in the bowl of a stand mixer fitted with the paddle attachment. Beat on medium speed until well mixed, scraping the sides of the bowl if needed. Turn the speed down to low, add both cheeses, and mix to combine.

Cover and refrigerate for at least 1 hour. You can make this up to 1 week ahead and store in an airtight container in the refrigerator.

To serve: Transfer the biscuit crackers from the wire rack to a serving platter. Transfer the dip to a serving bowl and serve alongside the crackers.

Carla's on television often, talking about food, and she's lived in Paris, but her roots are in Nashville. That's what led me to Starlito, one of the city's current biggest hip-hop exports. Starlito likes to title his albums after food, especially fowl: he's put out *Cold Turkey*, *Fried Turkey*, and *Hot Chicken*, among others. I sent her "Family to Feed," which is more a song about what a man has to do, aboveboard and otherwise, to get money to feed his family. It's an illustration of the difference between eating to live and living to eat.

Serves: 6 to 8
Prep time: 20 minutes
Cook time: as long as your favorite
brand of pigs in a blanket take

Studio Standard (Cocktail Spread)
Tom Sachs

Because so much of Tom's artwork is about space, I knew I wanted to give him a space song to prompt his contribution to the potluck. I considered David Bowie's "Space Oddity," of course, but moved on from that: too much of a cliché. I considered Elton John's "Rocket Man," too, but it had the same problem, plus more recent Kim Jong-un overtones. I had a moment with A Tribe Called Quest's "The Space Program" (you feel it, y'all?) and Daft Punk's "Contact" (which incorporates Apollo 17 audio). In the end, the song that made the most sense was Billy Preston's "Outa-Space," the classic 1971 instrumental in which Billy ran a clavinet through a wah-wah pedal and got something tasty and spacy.

You can now own a Tom Sachs piece! His classic cocktail spread. Unlike his other works of art, once it's consumed, it's gone. Every party spread needs a mini hot dog.

- 1 box pigs in a blanket (your preferred brand)
- Del Maguey Mezcal, Chichicapa
- Del Maguey Mezcal, Tobala
- Dijon mustard
- Heinz ketchup
- Hellmann's mayonnaise
- 8 pack (8-ounce/240-ml cans) Schweppes Ginger Ale
- Lindt chocolate bar by Lindor
- ½ pound (227 g) Ibérico ham (from Despaña, or local gourmet grocer), sliced thin
- 1 (1-pound/454-g) piece of Jarlsberg cheese
- 1 bunch celery, cut into sticks, about ½ by 3 ½ inches (1 by 9 cm)
- 1 bunch carrots, peeled and cut into sticks, about ½ by 3 ½ inches (1 by 9 cm)
- 8 ounces (227 g) sugar snap peas or snow peas
- 1 bunch of radishes, picked from the victory garden, preferably

Preheat your oven to the temperature suggested on the box of pigs in a blanket. Bake according to directions and, when cool enough to handle (after about 5 minutes), place them in your "cocktail set-up" according to the drawing.

Set up the remaining ingredients just as in the picture. Replenish as necessary. Enjoy.

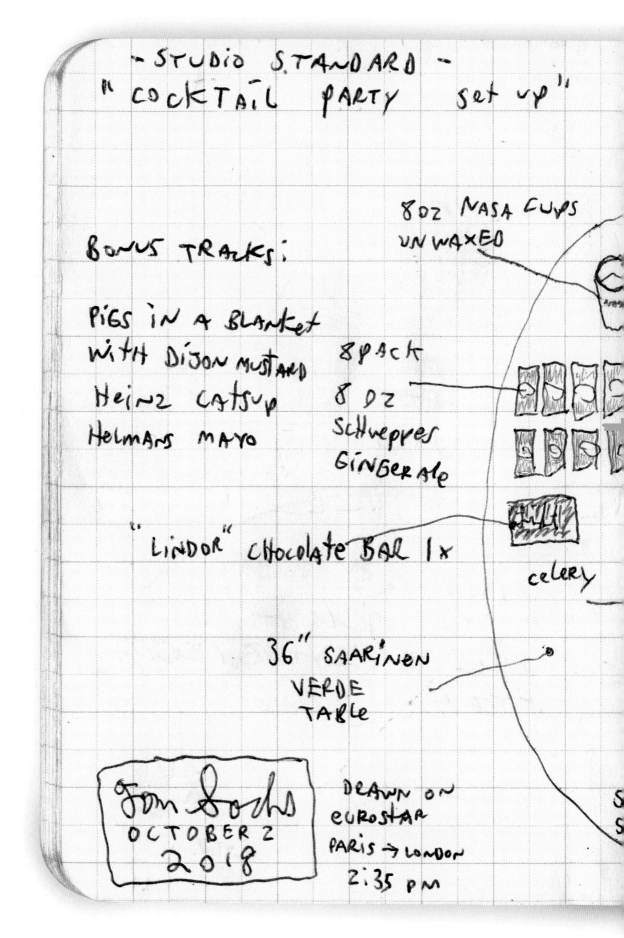

- STUDIO STANDARD -
"COCKTAIL PARTY set up"

8 OZ NASA CUPS
UNWAXED

BONUS TRACKS:

PIGS IN A BLANKET
WITH DIJON MUSTARD   8 PACK
HEINZ CATSUP   8 OZ
HELMANS MAYO   SCHWEPPES
                          GINGER ALE

celery

"LINDOR" CHOCOLATE BAR 1x

36" SAARINEN
VERDE
TABLE

Tom Sachs
OCTOBER 2
2018

DRAWN ON
EUROSTAR
PARIS → LONDON
2:35 PM

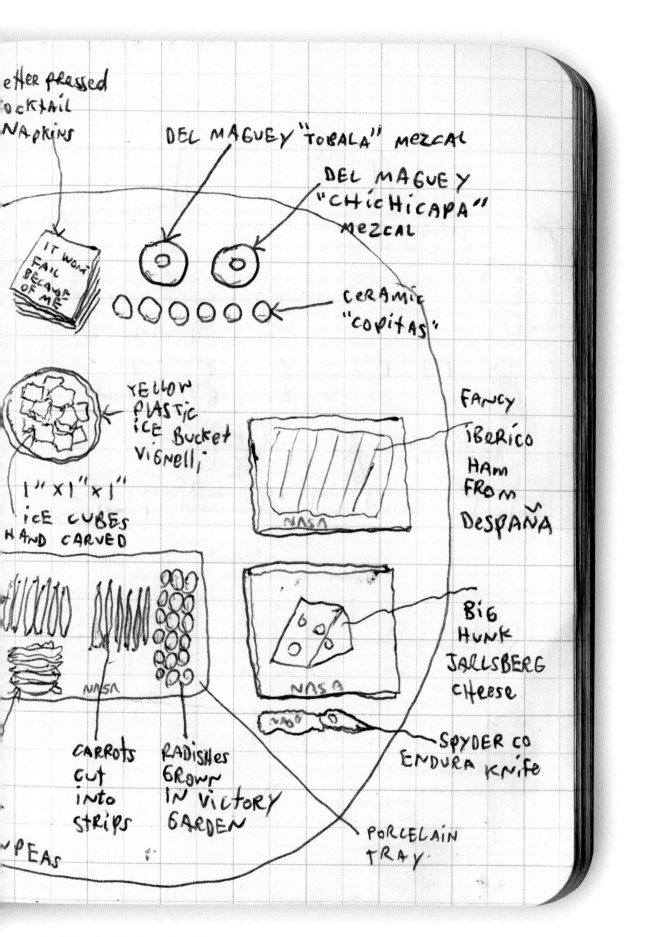

etter pressed
ocktail
Napkins

IT WONT
FAIL
BECAUSE
OF ME

DEL MAGUEY "TOBALA" MEZCAL

DEL MAGUEY
"CHICHICAPA"
MEZCAL

CERAMIC
"COPITAS"

YELLOW
PLASTIC
ICE Bucket
VIGNELLI

1" x 1" x 1"
ICE CUBES
HAND CARVED

NASA

FANCY
IBERICO
HAM
FROM
DESPAÑA

NASA

BIG
HUNK
JARLSBERG
CHEESE

SPYDER CO
ENDURA KNIFE

CARROTS
CUT
INTO
STRIPS

RADISHES
GROWN
IN VICTORY
GARDEN

PORCELAIN
TRAY.

PEAS

Plantains Two Ways
Fred Armisen

Serves: 10 to 12
Prep time: 10 minutes
Cook time: 20 minutes

Fred's dish uses two different kinds of plantains: yellow and green. They're not different plantains but the same plantain at different points of ripeness—green is at a harder and starchier stage (for making *tostones)*, and yellow is at a sweeter stage (for making *tajadas*). Plantains change and mature, like people, which is why it's the perfect dish for a group.

– 3 to 4 large ripe plantains
– ½ cup (120 ml) olive oil
– 1 ½ tablespoons kosher salt, plus more to taste

– 3 to 4 large green plantains
– Serve with your favorite hot sauce

To make the *tajadas* (the ripe, sweet plantain): Use a knife to score the plantains lengthwise to help release the skin. Slice the plantains on a bias, about ¾-inch (2-cm) thick.

Heat ¼ cup (60 ml) of the oil in a large skillet over medium heat until shimmering. Working in batches if needed, add the plantains to the skillet and cook for about 2 minutes on each side until they begin to turn golden brown. Turn them only once if possible.

Using a slotted spoon, remove the plantains from the skillet and onto a paper towel–lined plate. Season the plantains with 1 teaspoon of the salt while hot. Use the remaining oil in the pan to fry another batch using the same method as before and season again with salt.

To make the *tostones* (the green, savory kind): Use a sharp knife to separate the peel from the green plantains. Cut the plantains into very thin, straight slices. Add the remaining olive oil to the skillet and heat over medium. Add the plantains to the skillet and cook for about 3 minutes on each side, until light golden in color.

Using a slotted spoon, remove the plantains from the skillet to a flat surface such as a cutting board. Leave the skillet over the heat. Use a rolling pin or bottom of a clean pan to smash the plantains.

Return the plantains to the skillet and cook once more for about 1 minute on each side until the newly smashed plantain is golden brown. Using a slotted spoon, remove from the pan and season using the remaining salt to taste.

Serve immediately with your favorite hot sauce.

Fred is an innovator, confident no matter what creative risks he takes, so I picked Boogie Down Productions, "The Style You Haven't Done Yet." Even though KRS-One acted like he was older, he was still in his early twenties. "This style is for the gifted, poetically uplifted," he says, and he also says, "Don't you know that it's KRS-One that comes to sing the styles that ain't sung" (that's innovation and development). My favorite part comes at the end, when he says, "Oh gosh, dude. Oh gosh. Oh yes, dude. Oh yes." That's game recognizing game—in the mirror.

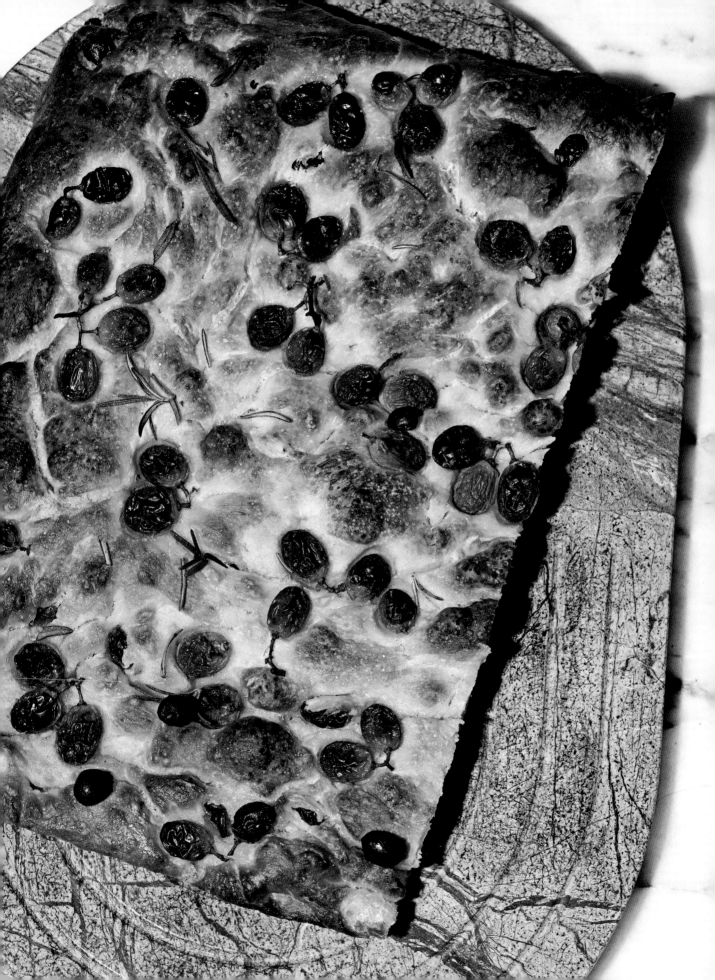

Grape Focaccia
Martha Stewart

Serves: 10 to 12
Prep time: 25 minutes,
plus 3 hours inactive time
Cook time: 40 minutes

The smell of bread and Martha Stewart almost go hand in hand. Martha's grape focaccia is so warm and welcoming—telepathically instructing guests to have a good time.

– 12 ounces (340 g) seedless grapes
  on the stem
– ⅓ cup plus 3 tablespoons (120 ml)
  extra-virgin olive oil, plus more for the pan
– 1 tablespoon plus 1 teaspoon kosher salt
– 4¾ cups (595 g) all-purpose flour
– ½ cup plus 2 tablespoons (95 g)
  golden raisins
– ¾ tsp active dry yeast
  (from one 1-ounce/28.35-g envelope)
– 2¼ cups (533 ml) warm water,
  between 95 and 105°F (35 and 40°C)
– 3 tablespoons sanding sugar
– 2 tablespoons fresh rosemary
– Flaky salt

Martha is the ultimate entertainer, and included under that broad umbrella is another title: she's the OG of potlucks. When you're throwing a dinner party, you want people to come through the door and be greeted by something made by Martha. There's no better way to establish the tone. I tried to think about what that would be: baked bread? A meticulously arranged cheese plate? Imagining what she would make was more difficult than picking a song to prompt her to make it. There was only one choice: a song by her partner in potlucks, Snoop Dogg: "Life of Da Party."

(recipe continues on following page)

Remove the large stems from the bunch of grapes, then break the bunch down into small clusters over a medium bowl. Place all of the small clusters and any loose grapes in a medium bowl, and toss the grapes with 1 tablespoon of the oil and ½ teaspoon of salt.

In the bowl of a stand mixer fitted with the dough hook attachment, mix together the flour, raisins, and yeast on low speed. Slowly add the warm water and continue to mix on low speed for 3 minutes until completely combined. Use a spatula to check the bottom of the mixing bowl making sure any remaining flour is incorporated. The dough will be very sticky.

Pour ⅓ cup (75 ml) oil into a large bowl or container with a lid. Add the dough and turn to coat. Cover the dough with a tight-fitting lid or plastic wrap. Place it in the warmest area of your kitchen for at least 2 hours or until doubled in size.

Preheat the oven to 450°F (230°C).

Oil an 18 by 13-inch (46 by 33-cm) baking sheet well and turn the dough out onto the prepared pan. Spread the dough out by pressing your fingertips into the dough. Leave out, uncovered, for 1 hour, or until the dough has once again doubled in size.

Drizzle the remaining 2 tablespoons oil over the dough, use your fingertips to dimple and stretch the dough to the corners of the pan.

Scatter the grapes over the top of the dough and sprinkle with the sanding sugar and rosemary. Finish with a few pinches of flaky salt.

Bake the focaccia for 20 minutes, then rotate the pan and bake for an additional 15 to 20 minutes, until golden brown. The grapes will begin to caramelize from the sugar; don't worry, they are delicious this way!

When cool enough to handle, transfer the bread from the pan to a wire rack to let cool at least 15 minutes. Slice into small squares and serve.

Guacamole
Dustin Yellin

Serves: 8 to 10
Prep time: 20 minutes
Cook time: None!

The simplest recipes are often the party hit. Dustin's guacamole illustrates this principle perfectly. His artwork may be complex to look at, but here the complexity is in the taste—Dustin adds a bit of chili powder for something special—but otherwise straightforward, easy to prepare, and easy to enjoy.

- 1 red onion, diced
- 1 tablespoon plus 1 teaspoon salt, plus more to taste
- 4 ripe avocados
- 1 bunch cilantro, tender stems and leaves picked
- 3 limes, juiced
- 1 serrano chile, finely diced
- ½ teaspoon chili powder
- ¼ teaspoon freshly ground black pepper
- Serve with tortilla chips

In a medium bowl, toss the red onion with 1 tablespoon of the salt and let sit for 10 minutes, tossing occasionally. This helps the onion release some sharpness and acidity. Drain the onions into a fine mesh sieve and rinse under cold water.

Halve the avocados and scoop the flesh into a medium bowl. Finely chop the cilantro and add to the bowl with the avocado. Add the onion, lime juice, serrano, 1 teaspoon salt, chili powder, and pepper and gently fold and mash together. Taste the guacamole and add more salt to balance the acid if necessary.

Serve with tortilla chips.

Dustin Yellin's art has always seemed to me to have a kinship with hip-hop. I don't know if he'd agree, at all, but the way he works—building layers of images on glass, and then combining them into something that has its own independent existence—reminds me of the way that hip-hop artists build songs. If you know what you're looking at, or where to look, you can decode his works and extract individual components. In that spirit, I found a song that was a perfect match: "Layers" by Royce da 5'9", a highly philosophical song about the workings of the hip-hop world. Between the verses, Royce has spoken interludes about creative inspiration, about ownership of creative product, and the trickiness of locating yourself in a legacy. It's a thoughtful song, and worthy of Dustin's art.

Serves: 6 to 8
Prep time: 10 minutes
Cook time: 15 minutes

Roasted Kale Chips
Ardenia Brown

Soul food used to be a survival diet. Now it's haute cuisine. The same thing happened with hip-hop, of course. We take what we like and make it a high-end product. Part of that trend is making healthier soul food and blending it with other influences. I have my own version of that process thanks to Ardenia, who has been my personal chef for a decade. She's not shielding me from the food of my youth. She's finding a version of it that works today. She updates and backdates all at the same time. Goodie Mob represented that idea well; they had one foot in traditional soul and another in the future. I sent her "Soul Food," the title track from their 1995 debut.

Ardenia's kale chips are the magical, healthy equivalent of collard greens; they are crispy, delicious, and a healthy snack awaiting your guests.

- 1 large or 2 small bunches lacinato kale, center rib removed
- 1 tablespoon Maldon salt
- 1 tablespoon lemon pepper
- 1½ teaspoons freshly gound black pepper, ground
- 1½ teaspoons dried thyme
- 1½ teaspoons dried rosemary
- 1 tablespoon ground turmeric
- 1 teaspoon ground ginger
- 1 teaspoon cayenne pepper
- 2 tablespoons toasted sesame seed oil

Preheat the oven to 400°F (205°C).

Wash the kale well, making sure to remove any dirt from the leaves. Pat dry, tear the leaves in half, and place in a large bowl.

In a small bowl, combine the salt, lemon pepper, black pepper, thyme, rosemary, turmeric, ginger, and cayenne.

Add the oil to the kale and massage the kale with your hands, making sure the leaves are nicely coated with the oil. Sprinkle with the spice mixture and toss to evenly coat.

Lay the kale leaves out on two baking sheets in a single layer, being careful not to overlap the leaves. Roast for 7 minutes, then use tongs to flip the kale leaves over and roast for another 7 minutes, or until the edges of the leaves just begin to turn golden brown. Allow the kale to cool for 10 minutes. Then, use tongs to transfer the kale to a serving bowl. If necessary, use the same baking sheet to roast another round of kale chips.

Jalapeño Salmon Fish Skins with Blistered Shishito Peppers
Ardenia Brown

Serves: 4 to 6
Prep time: 10 minutes
Cook Time: 15 minutes

These fish skins are a modern variation on pork rinds. Ask your local fish market if they have any skins available, or if they can set some aside. They're often available for cheap. And ask for them scaled.

For the Fish Skins:
– Skin from 2 sides of salmon, each approximately 12 inches (30.5 cm) long
– 3 tablespoons (45 ml) extra-virgin olive oil, divided
– 1 teaspoon jalapeño seasoning (can be purchased online)
– 1 tablespoon lemon pepper
– ¼ teaspoon cayenne pepper
– ½ teaspoon salt, plus more to taste

For the Shishito Peppers:
– 12 shishito peppers
– 1 tablespoon extra-virgin olive oil
– Salt, to taste

Serve with:
– ½ cup (35 g) microgreens, or soft herbs such as cilantro or parsley

Lay the salmon skin on a cutting board and pat both sides completely dry.

Cut the salmon skin into triangles a little larger than a tortilla chip.

In a small bowl, combine 2 tablespoons of oil and the remaining ingredients. Use a pastry brush to lightly brush the salmon skins with the spice mixture.

Place the shishito peppers in a large bowl with 1 tablespoon of oil and season with salt to taste. In a large nonstick frying pan over medium heat, add the peppers and oil and let them blister without burning, about 3 minutes. With a slotted spoon, remove the peppers and set aside.

Use the same frying pan to heat 1 tablespoon of oil. Add 3 to 4 pieces of salmon skin. They shouldn't overlap. Cook the skins 3 to 4 minutes per side until golden brown.

Use a slotted spatula to remove the skins from the pan. Season once more with salt and set them aside on a wire rack to cool.

Plate the peppers and skins together on a few small plates of your choosing.

START IT UP:

SMALL PLATES

At a restaurant, appetizers have to work in concert with the main course. You order something different, or something that you know will be complementary. At a dinner party, some guests might come early, eat like a trencherman, and then leave. Other people might miss the first course entirely. You can't control that kind of thing. For that reason, I like to have all kinds of appetizers available: traditional complements, but also appetizers that are a little more filling, and those that can sit on a table a little longer.

Serves: 8 to 10
Prep time: 10 minutes
Cook time: 10 minutes

Chickpea and Spinach Tapas
Padma Lakshmi

Padma is not only a foodie but a food writer, which means that she has done deep dives into several areas of the food world. She's a nerd, and I say that with great affection and nerd fellowship. One of the areas she explored was spices. She wrote a whole encyclopedia about them. In that spirit, I thought of the Red Hot Peppers—not the California rock band, but the hot eight-piece (sometimes seven) that Jelly Roll Morton led in the 1920s. They helped create the recipe for jazz, one of the great American dishes. Padma gets "Red Hot Pepper Stomp," recorded in New York in December of 1928.

Padma emphasizes the importance of making the chickpeas from scratch. It's what makes this dish cookbook-worthy.

- 1 cup (185 g) chickpeas, soaked, drained, and rinsed
- 6 cups (1.5 L) water
- 1 (10-ounce/285-g) package frozen spinach, or 10 ounces fresh spinach
- 1 red bell pepper, finely chopped
- 1 tablespoon finely diced chives
- Juice of 2 lemons (about 4 tablespoons/60 ml)
- ⅓ cup (75 ml) extra virgin olive oil
- 1 teaspoon sumac
- 2 teaspoons salt
- Freshly ground black pepper
- Serve with flatbread or pita chips

For the chickpeas, soak a cup overnight. You can also use the quick-soaking method: cover with cold water, bring to a boil over medium heat, turn off the heat, cover, and leave for an hour. This will ensure the chickpeas cook evenly. Now it's time to cook the chickpeas. Place the chickpeas in a medium pot and cover them with the water.

If using frozen spinach, defrost the spinach according to the package instructions, squeeze out excess water, and chop it. If using fresh spinach, bring a medium pot of salted water to a boil and cook the spinach until just wilted, about 30 seconds. Drain in a colander and squeeze out excess water. Finely chop the spinach and then squeeze once more.

In a large bowl, combine the spinach, chickpeas, bell pepper, chives, lemon juice, oil, sumac, and salt. Season with black pepper.

Serve with flatbread, pita chips, or toasted bread.

Crab Rangoon
Greg Baxtrom

Serves: 10 to 12
Prep time: 20 minutes
Cook time: 15 minutes

This dish has the fine-dining background of Greg's culinary history with the accessibility of a crowd-pleasing dish for your potluck. For extra credit, grow your own kale. Do yourself a favor and head to your local grocery store for sweet & sour sauce!

- 1 tablespoon neutral oil, such as grapeseed
- 1 bunch kale, ribs removed, finely chopped
- 1 teaspoon salt, plus more to taste
- 1 cup (135 g) cooked crabmeat
- 1 cup (245 g) ricotta cheese
- 1 package store-bought wonton wrappers (at least 30 wrappers)
- 2 quarts (2 L) neutral oil, such as canola or vegetable, for frying

Heat the oil in a medium sauté pan over medium heat. Add the kale and season with salt. Cook until tender but still bright green, about 3 to 5 minutes. Turn the kale out into a large bowl to cool slightly. Then add the crab and ricotta. Season again to taste.

Lay out 10 wonton wrappers and distribute about 1 teaspoon of filling per wrapper. It's tempting to add more, but by doing so you risk your rangoon exploding during the cooking process.

Fill a small bowl with water, dip your fingers in the water, and then trace the border of the first wrapper. Bring all four corners of the wrapper to a point in the center, pressing to seal, and then follow the seams down toward the filling, pressing and sealing as you work. Dip your fingers in the water again and repeat the sealing process with the remaining wrappers. Set the completed rangoon aside as you work and repeat the process once more with the remaining wrappers.

Heat 2 quarts of oil over medium heat in a high-sided pot or Dutch oven. Bring the oil to 350°F (175°C). Working 4 to 5 at a time, fry in batches for about 3 minutes, until light golden in color. Use a slotted spoon or tongs to remove rangoon from the fry oil and let drain on a paper towel lined plate. Repeat the frying process. Serve with sweet and sour sauce.

Greg Baxtrom is the man behind Olmsted, a restaurant in the Brooklyn neighborhood of Prospect Heights. I stayed in the borough, though I went a few neighborhoods away, to Fort Greene, and to an artist who is deeply identified with the borough, Mos Def. When you pick a Mos Def song, you're picking something that's socially aware, brilliantly analytical, and also organized for maximum potency: sort of like good food. I sent Greg "Climb," a beautiful and abstract song about ambition, aspiration, loneliness, and community.

Perfect No-Roll Crab Roll

Ignacio Mattos

Serves: 8
Prep time: 15 minutes
Cook time: 25 minutes

I learned a new word through Ignacio's recipe: tomalley, which is the creamy orange part of the crab that some people call crab fat. It's a real delicacy, somewhere between uni and caviar. I also relearned an old trick, which is that people are really impressed by a ring mold.

For the Crab:
- 5 tablespoons (70 g) unsalted butter
- 6 ounces (170 g) Jonah or Dungeness crabmeat, cooked (you will need 1 to 2 whole crabs for this recipe)
- ¼ cup (85 g) crab tomalley
- Zest from ½ a lemon
- ½ cup (120 ml) white wine vinegar
- ½ cup (120 ml) chardonnay vinegar
- 6 or 7 strips dulse seaweed
- ½ cup (120 ml) kombu butter stock, warmed
- Grey salt (This can be purchased online or at most specialty food shops. It is a French salt that is grey from crystallizing on clay as it dries.)

For the Stock:
- 2 (3½-inch/9-cm) pieces kombu
- 1¾ ounces (50 g) dried shiitake mushrooms
- 5 tablespoons (70 g) unsalted butter
- Squeeze of fresh grapefruit juice
- Grey salt, to taste

Remember when the Beatles first arrived in America and they called it the British Invasion? Well, around the same time, bands from Uruguay arrived in Argentina and made a splash on their music scene. They called that the Uruguayan Invasion, which is a much more musical phrase. Ignacio Mattos is from Uruguay, which means that he has certainly heard of Los Shakers, one of the premier groups of the invasion, and their hit "Break It All." The song is a near-perfect example of how to take something that already existed (in this case, the Beatles' sound) and give it local flavor. It's also a song about fellowship and company, which are at the heart of both music and food: "You forget you're tired / You forget you're sad / Can I shake and dance / With friends tonight."

(recipe continues on following page)

For the crab: Melt the butter in a small saucepan over medium heat. Cook until it is light golden in color and smells nutty, about 3 minutes.

Remove the butter from the heat and pour it into a small bowl. As the butter cools, the darker bits will sink to the bottom of the bowl.

In a medium bowl, gently fold the crabmeat and its tomalley together, being careful not to break up the tomalley. Zest the lemon over the crab and add most of the brown butter, leaving behind the dark bits on the bottom of the bowl.

Combine the vinegars. Then place the dulse in the vinegar mixture and let it soften for 30 seconds. Drain the dulse well, add it to the crab mixture, and gently combine. Discard the vinegars.

For the kombu stock: Soak the kombu in a bowl of hot water for about 5 minutes to remove excess salt and then drain.

Place the kombu and shiitakes in a small pot. Add 2 cups (500 ml) water and place over medium heat, bringing the stock to a simmer. Reduce the heat to low and very gently cook for 20 minutes.

Strain the stock through a fine-mesh strainer into a bowl and then return it to the pot. Add the butter and melt it in over low heat. Use an immersion blender to incorporate the butter.

Finish the stock with a squeeze of fresh grapefruit and season with two pinches of salt. You will have extra stock from this recipe; use it as the stock for a recipe that calls for broth.

To serve: Place a ring mold in the center of a serving plate and spoon in half of the crab mixture. Remove the ring mold and repeat on a second plate with the remaining crab. Pour 2 tablespoons of the stock on each portion and finish with a pinch of grey salt.

Poached Chicken Wraps
Camille Becerra

Serves: 8 to 10
Prep time: 20 minutes
Cook time: 25 minutes

When someone brings a "make your own" dish to a party, they are helping out the host. Some decisions are already made, like how to chop ingredients, and the rest of the participation is fun for everyone at the party. Encourage potluck contributions like this one. They're halfway between dishes and games. Also, this was arguably the healthiest thing at my potluck, and will arguably be the healthiest thing at yours.

For the Chicken:
- 4 (8-ounce/227-g) skinless boneless chicken breasts
- 2 tablespoons salt, plus more to taste
- 3 cups (710 ml) water
- 2 cups (480 ml) dry white wine
- ½ cup (120 ml) distilled white vinegar
- 1 head garlic, halved
- 1 small onion, sliced
- 2 stalks lemongrass, halved and pounded to crush
- 1 (1-inch/2.5-cm) piece ginger, thinly sliced
- 1 cinnamon stick
- 3 bay leaves
- 1 dried red chile, such as chile de árbol or bird's eye chile

For the Chili Sauce:
- 3 teaspoons toasted sesame seeds
- ¼ cup (60 ml) tahini
- 1 clove garlic, peeled
- 1 1½-inch (4-cm) piece ginger, peeled and sliced
- 1 tablespoon chili garlic sauce (tuong ot toi)
- ¾ cup (180 ml) water
- 1 teaspoon soy sauce
- 1 tablespoon rice vinegar
- 1 teaspoon fish sauce
- 1 tablespoon toasted sesame oil

For Serving:
- 3 to 4 heads of lettuce such as butter, Little Gem, Castelfranco, radicchio, or escarole
- 2 teaspoons sesame seeds
- 1 bunch cilantro
- 1 bunch mint
- 2 cups (110 g) mixed sprouts, such as sprouted mung beans, radish sprouts, or pea shoots
- 1 cup (135 g) roasted salted peanuts, chopped
- garlic sauce (tuong ot toi)

Bill Evans developed most of the vocabulary for contemporary jazz piano. He worked with Chet Baker, with Scott LaFaro, and most famously with Miles Davis. His time with Davis yielded *Kind of Blue*, arguably the most famous jazz album of all time. One of the signal moments on that record is "Blue in Green," and over the years it's become clear that the tune mostly came from Evans. I picked that song for Camille Becerra because I imagined that she would make something healthy and subdued and beautiful.

(recipe continues on following page)

To make the chicken: Season the chicken generously with salt. Leave the chicken out while you make the poaching broth.

Combine the water, wine, vinegar, garlic, onion, lemongrass, ginger, cinnamon, bay leaves, red chile, and salt in a large pot over medium heat. Bring to a simmer and cook for 15 minutes.

Add the chicken and adjust the heat to maintain a simmer. Cover and cook for 7 to 10 minutes. To check if chicken is ready, remove one chicken breast from the pot and cut in half; the center should not look raw but should still have a slightly pink center. The chicken will continue to cook as it cools.

Use a slotted spoon or tongs to remove the chicken from the broth to a cutting board. When cool enough to handle, thinly slice it.

To make the sauce: Set aside 2 teaspoons sesame seed for garnish in a small bowl. Combine all of the ingredients for the chili sauce in a blender and blend until completely smooth, scraping down the sides if necessary.

To serve: Lay out the lettuces, chicories, herbs, seeds, sauces, and sprouts in small dishes or directly on a platter. Encourage people to make their own wraps with the garnishes, and don't forget the sauce.

Sweet Potato Kimchi Pancake

Nyesha Arrington

Serves: 15 to 20
Prep time: 20 minutes
Cook time: 20 minutes

This dish is actually a great introduction to kimchi, both for those who shy away from it and those who don't know how they feel about it. The sweet offsets the sour and spice while creating a well-balanced pancake you wanna stack high on your plate.

- 4 scallions
- ½ cup (70 g) gluten-free flour, such as Cup4Cup
- ⅓ cup (43 g) cornstarch
- ½ teaspoon baking powder
- 2 tablespoons Korean red chili flakes
- 1 teaspoon kosher salt, plus more to taste
- 2 large eggs
- 1 tablespoon toasted sesame oil
- 1 tablespoon fish sauce
- 1 pound (454 g) Yukon Gold potatoes, peeled and coarsely grated
- 1 pound (454 g) sweet potatoes, peeled and coarsely shredded
- 1 cup (150 g) kimchi, roughly chopped
- 2 tablespoons neutral oil, such as vegetable or canola, plus more as needed
- Store-bought jujube sauce and crème fraîche

Cut the scallions into 1½-inch (4-cm) segments, then thinly slice them lengthwise so they resemble matchsticks.

In a medium bowl, whisk together the flour, cornstarch, baking powder, chili flakes, and salt.

In a large bowl, whisk together the eggs, sesame oil, and fish sauce. Whisk the flour mixture into the wet ingredients, then fold in the Yukon Gold potatoes, sweet potatoes, kimchi, and scallions.

Heat 1 tablespoon of the neutral oil in a large nonstick skillet over medium heat. Use a ⅓ cup (75 ml) measure or large spoon to make 3-inch (7.5-cm)-wide pancakes, fitting in as many as you can at a time without overcrowding your skillet. Cook for about 2 minutes on each side, until lightly browned and cooked through. Place on a wire rack and season with salt. Repeat the cooking process, adding oil by the tablespoon as needed, until you run out of batter. Serve with jujube sauce, crème fraîche, and more scallions.

Nyesha is an expert at fusing food and place and then building narratives around that fusion. Most of her stories are about Los Angeles, which meant that I tried to pick an LA story also. That sparked a memory of the first time I visited California, back in the mid-eighties, and specifically a memory of Toddy Tee's "Batterram," an early hip-hop song about the LAPD's use of a modified Army tank to break down doors in search of crack dealers. That's a completely different kind of cooking, but that's not why I picked it. To me, it was one of the first true signs that there was distinct a West Coast culture that wasn't making its way back east unless people brought it.

New Orleans–Style BBQ Shrimp and Burrata Toast
Kelly Fields

Serves: 10 to 12
Prep time: 15 minutes
Cook time: 40 minutes

Two things about this dish. First, the sauce can be prepared early—it stores for up to three days. The second thing is that not everyone is accustomed to shrimp heads. Encourage your guests to try them. It's worth it to get a little messy. Oh, wait, there is a third thing: despite what you may have been told, seafood and cheese do go together.

For the BBQ Sauce:
– 1 pound (454 g) large head-on shrimp, peeled, shrimp and shells reserved
– ⅓ cup (75 ml) olive oil
– 3 cups (720 ml) Worcestershire sauce
– 2 tablespoons freshly ground black pepper
– 2 tablespoons Creole seasoning
– 3 whole cloves
– 1 teaspoon salt
– 2 bay leaves
– Juice of 2 lemons (about 4 tablespoons/60 ml)

For the BBQ Shrimp:
– 2 tablespoons olive oil
– 3 cloves garlic, finely chopped
– 1 pound (454 g) head-on shrimp, plus shrimp reserved from the sauce recipe above
– 1½ cups (355 ml) BBQ Sauce
– 1½ cups (3 sticks/340 g) unsalted butter, diced
– Salt and pepper, to taste
– Juice of 1 lemon (about 2 tablespoons)

For the toast:
– 1 loaf of your favorite sourdough bread
– 3 tablespoons olive oil
– 1 pound (454 g) burrata cheese (two 8-ounce/227-g balls)
– 1 teaspoon flaky salt

Back in June of 2005, the Roots were in New Orleans, and we saw a band called the To Be Continued Brass Band, or TBC Brass Band, made up of teenagers from the Seventh and Ninth Wards. We hit it off with them and decided that we would make a record with them. It would be like collaborating with our younger selves, like looking at (and, in some ways, through) a mirror. Hurricane Katrina interfered, and the city changed, but Kelly has cooked in New Orleans, so I wanted to send her a song that reminded me of the city and the themes that have dominated the last decade: hope, challenge, resilience, local flavor, spirit, sauce, discovery, and rediscovery. I selected a live performance of "Let's Go Get Em," played live at Bourbon and Canal in honor of Brandon Franklin, a band member who was killed in 2010.

(recipe continues on following page)

To make the BBQ sauce: Remove the heads from the shrimp and set aside the bodies, shell on. Heat the oil in a medium saucepan over medium heat. Add the shrimp heads and cook until bright, about 2 minutes.

Add the remaining ingredients and cook on medium for about 20 minutes; the sauce should be at a strong simmer. Cook until sauce is reduced by half and begins to look sticky. Strain through a fine-mesh strainer and set aside.

To make the BBQ shrimp: Heat a large sauté pan over medium-high heat. Add the oil and garlic and cook just until the garlic begins to soften, about 30 seconds.

Add all the shrimp and cook 2 to 3 minutes, until bright red on both sides. Add the BBQ sauce and bring to a simmer for about 3 minutes until the shrimp are cooked through. Add the butter a little at a time, stirring it in as you go. Once the butter is incorporated, add the salt, pepper, and lemon juice. Taste and adjust the seasoning as needed.

For the toast: Heat a grill or grill pan over medium-high heat and preheat the broiler.

Cut the bread into 1-inch-(2.5-cm-)thick slices. Brush both sides with oil and grill on each side until charred to your liking.

Place the ball of burrata in a bowl and snip the top to release the inside. Stir the cheese together, breaking up the exterior and making a spreadable mixture.

Spread the burrata on the grilled bread and place on a baking sheet. Broil until the cheese melts and begins to bubble.

To serve: Place the grilled cheesy bread on a serving platter. Place the shrimp with the BBQ sauce in a bowl and invite guests to top their own toast. Make sure to leave an empty bowl for shells and plenty of napkins.

BRING IT RIGHT

SOUPS AND

ON OVER!
STEWS

Throughout this potluck—and really, anytime I'm around food—I'm always thinking about musical equivalents to different kinds of dishes. What is a cover song? What is a melody in need of lyrics? A soup or stew is about the closest thing I can think of to a great jam session. There are a lot of ingredients that mix and play together in the same pot. Eventually something delicious and unforgettable emerges. And a good soup or stew can go on forever, serving everyone in the room.

Chocolate Chili

Maya Rudolph

Serves: 8 to 10
Prep time: 20 minutes
Cook time: 2 ½ hours

If I didn't love Maya enough already, I fell head over heels in love with her all over again because of her chili. Anyone who combines chocolate chips and Fritos is a hero. Be a hero yourself. Bring her dish to your next potluck.

– 1 tablespoon vegetable oil
– 1 large yellow onion, diced
– 2 cloves garlic, finely chopped
– 2 tablespoons chili powder
– 1 tablespoon ground cumin
– 2 bay leaves
– 1 (15-ounce/425-g) can kidney beans, drained and rinsed
– 1 (15-ounce/425-g) can pinto beans, drained and rinsed
– 1 (15-ounce/425-g) can black beans, drained and rinsed
– 1 (15-ounce/425-g) can white beans, drained and rinsed

– 1 (28-ounce/794-g) can diced tomatoes with juices
– 2 (15-ounce/465-ml) cans tomato juice
– 2 teaspoons kosher salt, plus more to taste

For Serving:
– Chocolate chips
– Plain Greek yogurt
– Grated Cheddar cheese
– Sliced scallions
– Fritos
– Lime wedges
– Cholula or another hot sauce

Heat 1 tablespoon of the oil in a large Dutch oven or other heavy-bottomed large pot over medium heat until shimmering. Add the onion and cook for about 3 minutes, until translucent. Add the garlic and cook for 1 minute, or until fragrant. Transfer to a slow cooker. If you don't have a slow cooker, you can easily make this dish on your stovetop or in your oven (see Note).

Add the remaining ingredients to the slow cooker, stir well, cover, and cook on low for 2 hours.

Set out the chocolate chips and all other garnishes and let guests help themselves.

Note: For stovetop: Once all the ingredients are added to the Dutch oven, cook on low heat for about an hour, stirring occasionally to ensure nothing is sticking.

For oven: Preheat oven to 250°F (120°C). In an oven-safe pot, cook the chili uncovered for 1 to 1½ hours, stirring occasionally to ensure nothing is sticking.

Maya has a great story about Stevie Wonder and her mother, the singer Minnie Riperton. This was in Los Angeles, and when Stevie came by to present Minnie with the final mix of "Lovin' You," he stopped by Roscoe's first. Then he called from his car phone. "Come on out and listen to this," he said. "I've got a bucket of chicken out here." Food and music have been part of Maya's life since then, at least, intertwined, and she's carried that same joy and enthusiasm forward a generation. She got "Herbert Harper's Free Press News" by Muddy Waters. The song's from the 1969 album *Electric Mud,* which paired Muddy with younger funk-rock musicians, many of whom were members of Rotary Connection, Minnie Riperton's first band. The song is a strange brew of youthful energy and veteran confidence.

Serves: 14 to 16
Prep time: 20 minutes
Cook time: 3 hours, inactive

Shep's Maui Onion and Ginger Soup
Shep Gordon

Shep is a legendary manager and also a great host: I've been to many dinner parties at his home. But I also think of Shep as a figure of relaxation. He has cultivated that mind-set, and I have been lucky enough to spend time at his home in Maui, walking on the beach, resting, trying to reset my brain so I can dive back into the world of demands and deadlines. That's what I want my dinner parties to do: give people an oasis where they can recharge. I matched Shep with a song by Son of Bazerk, a Long Island–based rapper in the eighties who hooked up with Hank Shocklee, the architect of the Bomb Squad. The first Son of Bazerk album is a minor classic, and the lead single from the record, "Change the Style," is literally about switching channels and rhythms, sitting out for a contemplative moment before diving back in.

This dish is going to transport you. I knew Shep would bring a dish from his happy place. A dish that is the center of great conversations, laughter, and friends. This soup could feed an army, I assume: I didn't have an army, but it served everyone at the potluck. And the best part is that you can freeze the leftovers in a zip-top bag and take yourself back to that happy place anytime you want for up to three months.

– ½ cup (1 stick/113 g) unsalted butter
– 12 Maui onions, sliced
– 4-inch (10-cm) piece ginger, peeled and grated
– 2 tablespoons salt, plus more to taste
– 10 cups (2.5 L) chicken stock
– 1 (750-ml) bottle dry white wine
– 9 sprigs thyme
– 2 cups (480 ml) half-and-half
– Freshly ground black pepper
– 2 whole crabs, cooked and picked, for serving (optional)

In a very large stockpot (you may need to divide the recipe into two pots) melt the butter over medium heat. Add the onions, ginger, and salt. Reduce the heat to low and cook 15 to 20 minutes, until the onions are soft, but try to avoid burning.

Add the chicken stock, wine, and thyme, increase the heat to high, and bring to a boil. Reduce the heat to low so it stays at a simmer and cook with the lid slightly ajar for 3 hours.

Remove the thyme stems, letting any leaves that fell off remain. Use a blender or immersion blender to puree the soup, working in batches if necessary.

If using a blender, return the soup to the pot and add the half-and-half. Season with salt and pepper.

Serve with the crab for that "wow" factor, if you like.

Serves: 8 to 10
Prep time: 20 minutes
Cook time: 25 minutes

South Philly Seafood Stew
Tariq Trotter

Tariq has been my musical partner for decades—in the Roots, at Fallon—and is one of the best cooks I know, although he keeps it close to the vest and personal. It's for him and his family, something he does because he likes eating fine food, and he doesn't really care about getting noticed or getting credit. On the other hand, sometimes he will show up at work with something he cooked, and it'll be amazing, like it came from the hands of a professional. Lambert, Hendricks, and Ross's "Home Cookin'" has the same mix of smooth professionalism and vocal daring.

The Roots got our start in Philly, playing out on South Street. Instead of a drum, I used a chitlin bucket. Tariq brought everything back home with a local favorite. Some call this cioppino, and there are variations around the country (San Francisco, for example), but I think of it, always and forever, as Philly stew.

- 3 tablespoons olive oil
- 1 Spanish onion, roughly chopped
- 1 bulb fennel, thinly sliced
- 2 medium shallots, diced
- 5 cloves garlic, finely chopped
- 2 teaspoons kosher salt, plus more to taste
- 2 teaspoons red chili flakes
- 1½ cups (375 ml) vermouth or white wine
- ¼ cup tomato paste
- 1 (28-ounce/794-g) can whole peeled San Marzano tomatoes
- 1 (32-ounce/907-g) box seafood stock
- 2 bay leaves
- 1 pound (454 g) mussels
- 1 pound (454 g) clams, soaked in water to cover for 2 hours to purge the sand
- 1 pound (454 g) white fish, such as halibut or turbot
- 1 pound (454 g) large wild shrimp, peeled and deveined
- 1 pound (454 g) scallops
- White pepper, to taste
- 1 nice lump Parmesan cheese, about 4 ounces (113 g)
- Toasted Italian bread

Heat the oil in a large Dutch oven or other heavy-bottomed large pot over medium-high heat. Add the onion, fennel, shallots, and garlic and cook until beginning to caramelize, about 8 to 12 minutes. Add the salt and red chili flakes.

Add the vermouth and cook for 1 minute to deglaze the pan. Add the tomato paste and stir until completely combined.

Add the tomatoes, stock, and bay leaves, and stir well. Bring to a strong simmer, then add the mussels and clams, cover and cook until they open, 3 to 5 minutes. Using tongs, remove the mussels and clams to a bowl.

Return the broth to a simmer. Add the fish, shrimp, and scallops and cook until just cooked through, about 5 minutes. Return the mussels and clams and all of their liquor to the pot and season with salt if needed.

Transfer to a serving bowl and crack some white pepper over the top. Serve with grated Parmesan cheese and toasted Italian bread.

Mexican Corn Chowder
(There Is No Such Thing)
Alex Stupak

Serves: 10 to 12
Prep time: 35 minutes
Cook time: About 5 hours
(mostly inactive)

Alex was generous with the corn chips, which layer over the rest of the soup and protect its taste and temperature. Oh, also, don't forget the lime: you're supposed to squeeze it over your soup. It gives the whole experience a kick. Alex served this in what he called "dorm style," on a hot plate. I guess that's not the only way to do it, but it worked.

- 1 (6-ounce/170-g) piece smoky bacon, diced (about ¾ cup)
- 6 ounces (170 g) fresh Mexican chorizo, removed from the casing (about ¾ cup)
- ½ cup (1 stick/115 g) unsalted butter
- 2 medium white onions, diced
- 1 bunch celery, diced
- 1 tablespoon kosher salt, plus more to taste
- 8 cups (2 L) water
- 8 ounces (227 g) fresh corn masa for tortillas, or 1 cup (116 g) masa harina (preferably from Bob's Red Mill)
- 2 pounds (908 g) boneless pork shoulder, cut into 1-inch (4-cm) pieces
- 3 pounds (1.4 kg) fresh sweet corn kernels (about 8 cups)
- 2 cups (480 ml) heavy cream

For Serving:
- 1 bunch cilantro, tender stems and leaves roughly chopped
- 1 (8-ounce/227-g) bag tortilla chips, broken into large pieces
- Mexican hot sauce, like Cholula or Valentina
- 4 limes, each cut into 8 wedges

Alex is, among other things, a visionary of Mexican cuisine. I matched him with "Es Mi Gusto" by Akwid, an innovative Mexican American hip-hop act that raps over traditional Mexican music beds, heavy on the brass. Plus, even though the title translates to "It's my pleasure," it also translates to "It's my taste." In a perfect world, a dish you bring to a potluck is both of these things.

(recipe continues on following page)

Heat a large Dutch oven or other heavy-bottomed large pot over low heat and add the bacon. Once it has rendered a few tablespoons of fat, increase the heat to medium and cook until it is crispy and golden brown, about 7 to 10 minutes. Use a slotted spoon to transfer the bacon to a small bowl, leaving the fat in the pot.

Add the chorizo to the pot and cook, breaking it into smaller pieces, until golden brown, about 5 to 7 minutes. Use the slotted spoon, remove the chorizo from the pot and add it to the bowl with the bacon. Remove the grease from the pot and save it for another use. It has tons of flavor, but we don't want it to stain our chowder an odd color.

Keep the pot over low heat, add the butter, and let it melt. Add the onions, celery, and salt and sweat the vegetables until they are tender but not browned, about 12 to 14 minutes.

Combine the water and masa in a blender and blend until smooth. Add the mixture to the pot with the aromatics and adjust the heat to medium to bring to a simmer, stirring frequently so the masa doesn't stick.

Add the chunks of pork shoulder to the pot, cover, and simmer over low heat for 4 hours, stirring from time to time to make sure the masa doesn't stick to the bottom of the pot and burn. Taste a piece of the pork to make sure it is as tender as you want it to be; if not, continue to cook until it is.

Add the corn kernels and cream and simmer very gently for 20 minutes to allow the flavors to meld. Taste it again to make sure you love it, then add the rendered bacon and chorizo to make you immediately love it more.

Ladle the chowder into bowls and set up little bowls with the cilantro, crushed tortilla chips, and limes. Place them at the table along with the bottle of hot sauce and encourage everyone to garnish to their liking.

Mom's Chicken Curry
Lilly Singh

Serves: 10 to 12
Prep time: 15 minutes
Cook time: 1 hour

One of my favorite things about Lilly's dish is the color palette. She brought the dish in a pot that reminded me of the earth, with the red of the curry and the green of the herbs leaping up out of it. Growing up, this was Lilly's favorite meal of her mom's.

- 3 tablespoons oil, such as grapeseed, avocado, or coconut
- 3 large onions, diced
- 2 tablespoons finely diced garlic
- 3 tablespoons finely diced ginger
- 1 teaspoon cumin seeds
- 2 serrano chiles, seeded and diced
- 2 teaspoons ground turmeric
- ½ teaspoon red chili flakes, plus more to taste
- 2 teaspoons salt, or to taste
- 1½ cups (360 ml) water
- 2 beefsteak tomatoes, chopped
- 1 whole chicken, skin removed, cut into 10 to 12 pieces
- Basmati rice or pita bread
- ½ bunch fresh cilantro, tender stems and leaves picked

Heat the oil in a large Dutch oven or other heavy-bottomed pot over medium heat.

Add the onions and cook until golden brown, about 5 to 7 minutes. Add the garlic, ginger, and cumin and cook, stirring until aromatic, about 1 minute.

Add the serranos, turmeric, red chili flakes, and salt and stir well. Add the water and the tomatoes; simmer for 30 minutes, allowing the sauce to reduce and the flavors to meld. Add the chicken, return to a simmer, and cook for 10 minutes. Check to make sure there is enough liquid to cover the chicken at least halfway; if not, add more water. Cover and simmer for 30 minutes, or until the chicken is fork tender.

Season with salt if needed and serve over rice or with pita, garnished with cilantro.

I've been a big fan of Lilly and even had the chance to chat with her about her own creative process. She talked about shaking up tradition and forging your own path. She is, as you all know, a *bawse*, having an immense amount of success creating content on her YouTube channel. She's also done some hip-hop songs with a friend of hers, Humble the Poet. But I decided to go to her Epic Rap Battle; she starred in Wonder Woman versus Stevie Wonder. She was Wonder Woman, obviously, and T-Pain was Stevie Wonder. I matched her with "Superwoman (Where Were You When I Needed You)," because it's a beautiful Stevie song with a beautiful melody, and because Lilly's YouTube alias isn't Wonder Woman. It's Superwoman.

RIGHT THERE

SIDES AND

NEXT TO IT: SALADS

Sides and salads do double-duty, especially at a potluck, where timelines cross. They can be an extended stop for people who don't want to eat too much, or they can be a pause between courses for people who have committed to the entire dining experience. For me, they're also an opportunity for spicing things up visually: sides and salads mean lots of small plates circulating quickly around the room, so you can try out interesting colors and designs. Don't over-think it, but don't underthink it either.

Bok Choy and Cucumber Salad
Zooey Deschanel

Serves: 8 to 10
Prep time: 5 minutes

This recipe from Zooey comes together very quickly. If you only have ten minutes to get something green onto a table, this is your answer. The salad only gets better after an hour or two, so leave it out before guests arrive. And make sure the sesame oil is toasted.

- 3 heads bok choy, stems and leaves thinly sliced crosswise
- 3 Persian cucumbers, quartered and cut into ½-inch-(12-mm-) thick slices
- ¼ cup (60 ml) toasted sesame oil
- ¼ cup (60 ml) ponzu sauce
- 2 teaspoons salt
- 3 tablespoons sesame seeds, toasted

In a serving bowl, combine the bok choy and cucumbers.

In a small bowl, whisk the sesame oil, ponzu sauce, and salt.

Spoon the dressing over the salad and toss to combine. Top with the toasted sesame seeds and serve.

Zooey has a project called The Farm Project that's exactly what it sounds like, a way of reconnecting people with their food. Zooey also has a project called She & Him that's also exactly what it sounds like, a way of connecting her (and her musical partner, M. Ward: that's Him) to songs. To tie all that together, I thought about Prince's television appearance on Zooey's sitcom, *New Girl*, where her character performed a song with him ("FallInLove2Nite"), and then I thought further. I found another Prince song that works just as well to illustrate the idea of reconnecting people with their food: "Joint 2 Joint," off *Emancipation*. It's a long, multipart song, and in one of the parts Prince is eating breakfast, Cap'n Crunch with soy milk ("because cows are for calves"). I sent that.

Serves: 6 to 8
Prep time: 20 minutes
Cook time: 20 minutes

Peppers à la Famiglia Tomei
Marisa Tomei

Most people know Marisa Tomei from *My Cousin Vinny*, or *Slums of Beverly Hills*, or *Spider-Man: Homecoming*, but to me she'll always be Maggie on *A Different World*, the *Cosby Show* spinoff. I was in high school then, at a performing arts school in Philadelphia, and 1987 was the year that every kid wanted a Casio SK-1 sampler for Christmas. My future Rootsmate Tariq was in school with me, and I used to create beats on it for him to rap over. The SK-1 was famous because of a *Cosby Show* episode the previous February where the Huxtable kids got into a car accident with Stevie Wonder's limo. Stevie invited them down to the studio and ended up sampling a snippet of Theo's speech. That moment (known as the "Jammin' On the One" moment for what Theo says), is one of the central moments in the evolution of hip-hop. Denise was there, and then she went to college. I decided to send Marisa one of the songs that Tarik and I recreated on our SK-1: "Top Billin," by the Brooklyn duo Audio Two.

Marisa's dish is a family recipe that originated with her grandmother Rita and was passed down to Marisa and her brother, Adam (an LA pizzaiolo), among others in the family. It's easy to see why it has survived for all this time. The peppers can work on their own, or they can give extra energy to other dishes—you can put them on top of toast or next to your mac and cheese, and they'd be great alongside quiche.

– 8 large red peppers
– 5 medium cloves garlic, peeled and thinly sliced
– ¼ cup (60 ml) good extra-virgin olive oil, plus 1 tablespoon, divided
– Good sea salt, or flaky salt, such as Maldon
– Freshly ground black pepper
– 1 (28-ounce/794-g) can of San Marzano tomatoes

Preheat the oven to broil on the medium setting. Alternatively, you can fire up a grill to medium-high heat. Place the peppers over the heat and use tongs to turn the peppers every 3 to 5 minutes, until they become blackened on all sides.

Remove the peppers from the heat and place in a paper bag large enough that you can close it tightly.

After about 20 minutes, the peppers should be cool enough to handle. Working over a large bowl with a fine-mesh sieve placed on top, use a small knife to poke a hole in the bottom of each pepper and let the juices run into the bowl. Remove the seeds from all the peppers.

Use your hands to pull the charred skin off the pepper; it's okay if some very small bits of char remain.

Slice the peppers into ½-inch (12-mm) pieces and place in the mixing bowl with the juices. Add the garlic to the same bowl. Add the olive oil, toss gently, and season with salt and pepper to taste.

Empty the can of tomatoes and their juices into a Tupperware and pluck out four of the tomatoes. In a small sauté pan heat 1 tablespoon of oil over medium heat. Add the four tomatoes, crushing them with your hands as you add them to the pan. Season with salt and pepper and cook over medium heat for 15 minutes.

Add the tomatoes to the bowl with the peppers and check the seasoning again.

Herbed Shrimp Salad with Fried Green Tomatoes

Edouardo Jordan

Serves: 8 to 10
Prep time: 20 minutes
Cook time: 2 to 3 minutes

There was no shrimp salad in the Jill Scott song, but I was close. Edouardo's shrimp salad would be a hit at any picnic, including the indoor picnic of my potluck—or, for that matter, a Roots picnic. It's a perfect mix of flavor and texture.

For the Shrimp Salad:
- 2 pounds (908 g) fresh large shrimp, peeled, deveined, and blanched
- 2 tablespoons Dijon mustard
- ¼ cup (64 g) aioli or mayonnaise
- ¼ cup (6 g) picked parsley leaves, finely chopped
- 1 tablespoon tarragon leaves, finely chopped
- 3 tablespoons olive oil
- 4 stalks celery, leaves reserved, diced
- 1 small fennel bulb, fronds reserved, diced
- ½ red onion, finely diced
- 1 jalapeño pepper, seeds removed, finely chopped
- 1 teaspoon salt
- Leaves from 3 sprigs mint, finely chopped

For the Fried Green Tomatoes:
- 1 teaspoon kosher salt
- 3 cups (720 ml) buttermilk
- 3 cups (366 g) fine cornmeal
- 1 quart (950 ml) neutral oil, such as canola or vegetable oil
- 4 green tomatoes, sliced horizontally ¼ inch (6 mm) thick
- Flaky salt to finish

For Serving:
- 1 large head romaine lettuce
- 1 lemon, juiced (about 2 tablespoons)

Many chefs talk about their families as the basis for the way they cook: not just family recipes, but the process of people coming together to eat. That's the idea behind a potluck. For Edouardo, I picked Jill Scott's "Family Reunion." The song is a series of snapshots: Aunt Juicy calling Cousin Lonnie out for running around, Mickey and Steven fighting. Many scenes are centered on food. There's a barbecue grill, lemon cake of suspicious origin, and a cousin who brought her potato salad. I send that song, that photo album, to Edouardo.

(recipe continues on following page)

To make the shrimp salad: Cut the shrimp into thirds. In a large bowl, combine the mustard, aioli, parsley, and tarragon, then fold in the shrimp.

Heat a medium sauté pan over medium high-heat and add 1 tablespoon of the olive oil. Add the celery, fennel, red onion, and jalapeño and cook just until the edges begin to color, about 2 to 3 minutes. Season with salt, remove from the heat, and let cool.

Add the sautéed vegetables to the bowl with the shrimp and fold together. Add the fennel fronds, celery leaves, and mint.

To make the fried green tomatoes: In a medium bowl, whisk the salt and buttermilk together. Place the cornmeal in a small baking dish or plate.

Heat the oil in a large Dutch oven over medium heat. If you have a fry thermometer, use it! Heat the oil to 350°F (175°C). Add the green tomatoes to the buttermilk a few slices at a time, then dredge them in the cornmeal. Gently place them in the oil and fry until the tomatoes are a lightly browned, about 3 to 5 minutes.

Using a slotted spoon, remove the green tomatoes to a wire rack or paper towel–lined plate. Season with flaky salt.

To serve: Remove any tough outer leaves from the romaine and remove the root end. Break the romaine into leaves and halve or quarter any that are particularly large.

Place the leaves on a large platter and drizzle with the remaining 2 tablespoons olive oil and the lemon juice and sprinkle with flaky salt. Top with the shrimp salad and fried green tomatoes.

Serves: 6 to 8
Prep time: 10 minutes
Cook time: 3 minutes

Tomato Salad with Nectarines, Basil, and Bagna Cauda
Flynn McGarry

When I first met Flynn, he was fourteen and already a chef, cooking at pop-ups at his family's home in Southern California. He came to a few of my food salons and fit in perfectly with much older chefs. I decided to prompt Flynn with another teen star, or a pair of stars: the brothers Slim Jxmmi and Swae Lee, who record as Rae Sremmurd. They started as kids, making their art at home, and attracted the notice of producers and tastemakers. And then they released "Black Beatles," a huge hit that has a great lyric about being a prodigy: "Young bull, living like an old geezer."

Flynn's salad was young and energetic, just like Flynn. You can't go wrong with this balance of flavors and a pinch of good salt. That's right, good salt: I've learned that's one of the most important things you can have in your kitchen, or even that you can bring to someone else's kitchen. (As I've said elsewhere, when your recipe calls for a specialty condiment, you can bring it and leave it as a gift for your host.)

– 10 oil-packed anchovies, finely chopped
– 3 cloves garlic, grated
– 2 lemons, zested and then juiced (about 4 tablespoons/60 ml)
– 1 cup (240 ml) olive oil
– 2 large heirloom tomatoes, sliced
– 3 plums or nectarines, depending on the season
– 1 cup (40 g) fresh basil leaves, torn
– 1 tablespoon apple cider vinegar, or to taste
– Good flaky salt, such as Maldon

Combine the anchovies, grated garlic, lemon zest, and oil in a small saucepan and heat over medium until the mixture begins to fry and everything is fragrant, about 3 minutes. Remove from the heat and let cool.

Arrange the tomatoes, nectarines, and basil on a large serving platter. Squeeze the juice of the lemons over the salad, drizzle with the vinegar, and season with salt.

Spoon the dressing over the salad and toss gently, then add the remaining dressing and serve.

Serves: 8 to 10
Prep time: 20 minutes
Cook time: 30 minutes

Tomato/Potato Salad
Jessica Koslow

Jessica's restaurant, Sqirl, is one of LA's coolest treasures: laid-back and hip, with all the cachet you'd want. It's also a great place for breakfast. That's what everyone always told me, and it turned out to be true. For me, for many years, breakfast meant one thing and one thing only—cereal. I became kind of a connoisseur and even a collector; for a time, I was hell-bent on finding every last box of Cap'n Crunch Peanut Butter. Jessica's ideas about breakfast are much more sophisticated, but in thinking of her, in thinking of Sqirl, I got stuck on Method Man and Redman's "Cereal Killer."

Jessica, like me, hated tomatoes as a child. She has come a long way, and since this dish came into my life, I have, too. Tip: To keep the potatoes crispy, add them at the last minute.

For the Potatoes:
– **1 pound (454 g) Peewee potatoes, or preferred baby potato variety**
– **½ cup (120 ml) olive oil**
– **1½ teaspoons salt**

For the Cardamom Dressing:
– **1 teaspoon coriander seeds**
– **1 teaspoon cumin seeds**
– **½ cup (120 ml) rice vinegar**
– **⅓ cup (75 ml) apple cider vinegar**
– **1½ teaspoons ginger juice**
– **1 lemon, juiced (about 4 tablespoons/60 ml)**

– **1¼ teaspoons ground cardamom**
– **½ teaspoon kosher salt**

For Serving:
– **1¼ pounds (570 g) heirloom tomatoes, sliced ¾-inch (2-cm) thick**
– **1 tablespoon picked cilantro leaves**
– **1 tablespoon picked parsley leaves**
– **2 tablespoons thinly sliced red onion**
– **Flaky salt**
– **Fresh lemon juice**

Roast the potatoes: Preheat the oven to 425°F (220°C) and line a baking sheet with parchment.

Place the potatoes in a large bowl and toss with the oil to coat. Add the salt and toss again. Place on the prepared sheet and bake for 15 minutes.

Remove the potatoes from the oven and, using a small cast-iron pan or the bottom of a coffee mug, smash each potato until the skin begins to split. Use a spatula to gently toss the smashed potatoes and cook for 15 minutes, tossing once halfway through. Remove from the oven and cool while you compose the rest of the salad.

To make the dressing: Toast the coriander and cumin seeds in a small skillet over medium heat for about 30 seconds, until fragrant. Place in a spice grinder or mortar and pestle and grind to a medium fine powder. In a small bowl, whisk together the rice vinegar, cider vinegar, ginger juice, and lemon juice, then whisk in the ground coriander and cumin, the cardamom, and salt.

To assemble: Spoon some of the dressing on the bottom of a large serving platter along with half of the crispy potatoes and their oil. Follow with the tomatoes, picked herbs, red onion, more dressing, and the remaining potatoes and their oil. Finish with flaky salt and a squeeze of lemon.

VEG FRIE

YOU WANNA

NDS
IMPRESS

When I DJ, I'm always aware of the tension between expressing exactly what I want and serving the crowd. Hosting a potluck is similar. You can't stay in your own head. That means being aware of the dietary needs of the entire group, and some of those people are going to be vegetarians. (In fact, in recent years, I've been one of those people.) Don't forget about them. Give them plenty to eat, and plenty of choices—vegetarians aren't all about salads.

Easy Veggie Party Quiche
(That Will Blow Everyone's Minds)
Amy Poehler

Serves: 8
Prep time: 15 minutes
Cook time: 1 hour

Amy recommends not making your own piecrust, which saves time. Bonus: You can make a nice side salad by squeezing the juice from the lemon over some mixed greens.

- 1 (9-inch/23-cm) frozen piecrust
- 6 large eggs
- 1 cup (240 ml) heavy cream
- ¼ teaspoon ground or freshly grated nutmeg
- 3 sprigs thyme, leaves picked
- 1 teaspoon kosher salt, plus more to taste
- Freshly ground black pepper
- 8 ounces (227 g) Gruyère cheese, shredded
- 4 ounces (113 g) soft goat cheese

- 1 tablespoon unsalted butter, plus more as needed
- 2 cups (60 g) spinach, stemmed and roughly chopped
- 1 bunch asparagus, woody ends removed, cut into 1-inch (2.5-cm) pieces
- 8 ounces (227 g) mushrooms, such as button or cremini, thinly sliced
- 1 small onion, sliced
- 1 lemon, zested
- 5 sprigs fresh parsley, leaves picked

Preheat the oven to 325°F (160°C). Remove the pie crust from the freezer and place it on a baking sheet. Using a fork, poke a few holes into the bottom of the crust.

Place a piece of parchment in the bottom of the piecrust and cover it with pie weights, dried beans, or rice. Parbake the crust for 15 minutes, or until light golden brown. Place on a wire rack to cool and increase the oven temperature to 350°F (175°C).

Meanwhile, in a large bowl, whisk together the eggs, cream, nutmeg, thyme, salt, and pepper to taste. Fold in the Gruyère cheese and goat cheese.

Melt the butter in a medium sauté pan over medium-high heat. Add the spinach and a pinch of salt and stir until wilted. Remove the spinach from the pan to a bowl and set aside. Add another tablespoon of butter along with the asparagus, mushrooms, and onion and cook until softened and browned. Add to the plate with the spinach.

Fold the vegetables into the egg mixture, then pour into the parbaked crust. Bake for 40 to 45 minutes, until the top of the quiche is light golden brown and has puffed up.

Top with the lemon zest and parsley. Once cooled to room temperature wrap in a towel and bring to the party.

For Amy, I picked out Love Unlimited's "It May Be Winter Outside (But In My Heart It's Spring)." The song, cowritten by Barry White, is best known in its 1973 version by Love Unlimited, who were White's backup singers and then a spinoff group. This particular song reminds me of Amy because it harmonizes with something I have always thought about her. Amy's work—both her own comedy and other projects like Smart Girls at the Party—depends on identifying what's problematic about the world and making sure that people are able to feel comfortable anyway. It's an admirable pursuit, and as luck would have it, food does the same thing.

Open-Face Mushroom Sliders with Maple Chipotle Aioli
Haile Thomas

Serves: 12 to 16
Prep time: 25 minutes
Cook time: 50 minutes

Haile is an impressive young person who is an activist for healthy eating. She has talked about how her dad's history with diabetes encouraged her to move toward vegan cooking and speaking to young people about nutrition. Her mushroom sliders prove beyond a shadow of a doubt that recipes can leave out meat and still be every bit as satisfying and tasty. The mushrooms are so good that next time I might ask her to bring extras so I can eat them on their own.

Haile is a big deal in vegan cooking circles, already a national figure. She's also a kid, born in 2000. Thinking of 2000 makes me think of D'Angelo's *Voodoo*. I thought it would make sense to send Haile one of the songs from that record: "Chicken Grease," a song about getting the feel of music, about dancing, about the body and freedoms. I wanted to pass it along because the title works as a kind of challenge to vegan cooks (though really it's as much about a kind of funk guitar playing).

For the Lemon Cornbread:
- ½ cup (117 g) Earth Balance or other vegan butter, melted, plus more for greasing the pan
- 1 cup (125 g) all-purpose flour
- 1 cup (180 g) fine cornmeal
- ½ teaspoon baking soda
- 1 teaspoon baking powder
- ½ teaspoon salt
- 1 tablespoon fresh thyme leaves
- 2 tablespoons lemon zest
- ⅓ cup (83 ml) maple syrup
- 1 cup (240 ml) oat milk
- 1 tablespoon apple cider vinegar

For the Mushrooms:
- ½ cup (120 ml) oat milk
- ½ tablespoon fresh lemon juice
- 1 tablespoon Frank's RedHot sauce, or preferred hot sauce
- ½ cup (60 g) brown rice flour
- ½ cup (25 g) panko breadcrumbs
- 1½ teaspoons nutritional yeast
- 2 teaspoons kosher salt
- 1 teaspoon garlic powder
- 1 teaspoon onion powder
- ½ teaspoon freshly ground black pepper
- 1 teaspoon paprika
- ½ teaspoon ground chipotle
- ½ teaspoon ground turmeric

- ¼ teaspoon baking powder
- 8 ounces (227 g) mushrooms, such as maitake or oyster, torn gently into bite-size pieces
- ¼ cup (60 g) Earth Balance or other vegan butter, melted

For the Maple Chipotle Aioli:
- ¾ cup (192 g) vegan mayonnaise
- 2 cloves garlic, finely grated
- 1 teaspoon fresh lemon juice
- 1 tablespoon maple syrup
- 1 teaspoon ground chipotle
- 1 teaspoon paprika
- 1 teaspoon sea salt
- 3 sprigs fresh parsley, chopped
- Radish sprouts, for serving

(recipe continues on following page)

For the bread: Preheat the oven to 375°F (190°C). Lightly grease a loaf pan (8 by 4 by 2 ½ inches/20 by 10 by 6 cm) with vegan butter.

In a large bowl, whisk together the flour, cornmeal, baking soda, baking powder, salt, thyme leaves, and lemon zest.

In a small bowl, whisk together the melted vegan butter, maple syrup, oat milk, and vinegar.

Add the milk mixture to the dry ingredients and stir with a spatula to combine. Pour the batter into the prepared pan and bake for 30 minutes, or until the cornbread is golden and a toothpick or cake tester inserted in the center comes out clean. Cool in the pan on a wire rack for 15 minutes, then turn out onto the rack to cool completely.

For the mushrooms: Increase the oven temperature to 425°F (220°C) and place a baking sheet inside the oven to heat it up.

In a small bowl, whisk together the oat milk, lemon juice, and hot sauce. In a medium bowl, combine the rice flour, panko, nutritional yeast, salt, garlic powder, onion powder, black pepper, paprika, chipotle, turmeric, and baking powder. Toss the mushrooms in the milk mixture, then, one by one, dredge them in the flour mixture.

Remove the baking sheet from the oven and pour the melted vegan butter over the pan and swirl to coat. Place the mushrooms on the sheet, leaving a bit of space between them. Bake for 10 minutes, then flip the mushrooms and bake for an additional 12 minutes or until crispy and golden.

To make the aioli: In a food processor, combine all of the aioli ingredients and process until smooth.

To serve: Cut the bread into 1-inch slices and cut the slices in half so you have 16 slices. Swipe each slice of bread with the aioli and follow with a few pieces of fried mushroom and some radish sprouts.

Roasted Veggie Quinoa Bowl
Kimbal Musk

Serves: 8
Prep time: 35 minutes
Cook time: 45 minutes

If this book were a game show, I would have won the showcase showdown. Kimbal's bowl is in fact a garden: a healthy one, a delicious one, and one that elevated everyone's mood at the potluck.

For the Bowl:
– 3 cups (510 g) uncooked quinoa
– 6 cups (1.5 L) water
– 3 teaspoons kosher salt,
  plus more to taste
– 1 red bell pepper, chopped
– 1 head cauliflower,
  broken into florets
– 1 small bunch broccolini,
  trimmed
– 8 ounces (227 g) cremini
  mushrooms, quartered
– 1 red onion, chopped
– ½ cup (120 ml) extra-virgin
  olive oil, divided

For the Dressing:
– 1 bunch cilantro
– ½ cup (120 ml) canola oil
– ½ cup (120 ml) water
– 3 tablespoons tahini
– 2 lemons, juiced, about ½ cup
  (120 ml)
– 3 cloves garlic, peeled
– 2 teaspoons sriracha
– ¼ teaspoon ground coriander
– ¼ teaspoon ground cumin
– 1 teaspoon salt, plus more
  to taste

To Serve:
– Juice of 1 lemon
– ¼ cup (34 g) toasted sunflower
  seeds
– 2 tablespoons sesame seeds
– 1 bunch scallions, sliced into
  thin rings

Kimbal has built hundreds of gardens for schoolkids and launched Square Roots, an urban gardening accelerator in Brooklyn. I like the name: in fact, it was the original name of the Roots, though we had to give it up because there was another group using that name. Let me be clear: Kimbal had nothing to do with it. It was a folk group in Philly in the early nineties. But great minds think alike. In light of his work, I'm sending him Lenny Kravitz's "I Build This Garden for Us." Most people think the title is "I Built This Garden . . ." which would put the song in the past tense. But it's build. It's present. It's about an ever-present building.

Kimbal's tip:
Extra dressing can be
used as a dipping sauce.

(recipe continues on following page)

To make the bowl: Rinse the quinoa well in a mesh colander, then place it in a large pot and add the water and 1 teaspoon of the salt. Bring to a boil over medium-high heat, then decrease the heat to very low, cover, and cook for 15 minutes. Remove from the heat and let steam for 10 minutes, then fluff with a fork.

Preheat the broiler to medium-low. Divide the bell pepper, cauliflower, broccolini, mushrooms, and onion between 2 baking sheets and toss each with 3 tablespoons of the oil and 1 teaspoon of the salt. Broil the vegetables for 3 minutes, then rotate the sheets and broil for an additional 3 minutes, until charred. In a medium skillet, heat the remaining 5 table-spoons oil over medium heat until the oil is shimmering. Add 1 cup (200 g) of the cooked quinoa to the pan. Using the back of a heat-proof spatula spread the quinoa into an even layer. Let one side of the quinoa fry until it is golden brown, about 5 minutes, then use a spatula to flip the quinoa and fry the other side for about 5 more minutes. Remove the quinoa with a slotted spoon to a plate lined with paper towels. Season with salt while it's hot.

To make the dressing: Roughly chop half the bunch of cilantro place in the blender. Pick the leaves and tender stems from the remaining half and reserve for garnish.

Add the remaining dressing ingredients to the blender and blend on medium speed until smooth.

To serve: Place the quinoa on the bottom of a serving bowl. Toss with one quarter of the dressing. Follow with the roasted vegetables, drizzle with the lemon juice, and season with salt. Top with more of the dressing to your liking and follow with the toasted sunflower seeds, sesame seeds, fried quinoa, and scallions.

Spinach Pie
Natalie Portman

Serves: 8 to 10
Prep time: 20 minutes
Cook time: 20 minutes

My Beach Boys pick got me thinking about arrangement, and when Natalie's dish arrived, it surprised me in that regard. For starters, the visual organization—the tart is beautiful to look at. And I learned something, too, which is that phyllo dough is vegan.

- 8 ounces (227 g) store-bought phyllo dough
- ½ cup (120 ml) olive oil
- 1 yellow onion, thinly sliced
- 2 teaspoons salt, or to taste
- 4 cups (120 g) fresh baby spinach
- ¼ cup (34 g) pine nuts
- ¼ cup (35 g) golden or purple raisins
- Crumbled feta cheese, for serving (optional)

Preheat the oven to 400°F (205°C).

Remove the phyllo dough from the package and thaw according to the package instructions.

Use a pastry brush to coat the bottom and sides of a pie dish with the oil. Lay 1 phyllo sheet in the dish and brush with an even coating of oil. Repeat with the remaining sheets of phyllo, brushing each with oil.

Heat 2 tablespoons of the oil in a medium sauté pan over medium heat. Add the onion and 1 teaspoon of the salt and cook for about 5 minutes, until translucent and just beginning to turn golden on the edges.

Add the spinach and the remaining 1 tablespoon oil and stir until wilted. Add the pine nuts and raisins, then remove the pan from the heat and check the seasoning.

Fill the prepared pie dish with the spinach mixture. Use your hands to gently crimp the layers around the rim of the pie dish, leaving the center exposed.

Place on a baking sheet and bake for 20 to 25 minutes, until the edges of the phyllo are golden and crisp. Top with feta cheese, if using, and serve warm or at room temperature.

When I was younger, I used to have to conceal my Beach Boys obsession from other rappers. It was like hiding pornography. Brian Wilson, the leader of the Beach Boys, once ran a health-food store. That adds up to "Vegetables," a song from the ill-fated *Smiley Smile* record about . . . well, it's about eating vegetables. Nothing more complicated than that. Paul McCartney contributes percussion in the form of crunching celery. I give Natalie this song.

Serves: 10 to 12
Prep time: 20 minutes
Cook time: 1 hour

Whole Roasted Cauliflower with Two Sauces
Jessica Seinfeld

When Jessica cooks, she uses healthy ingredients but makes sure that everything tastes and looks pleasurable. She is also concerned with the origin of food. She does her own gardening and likes to talk about sourcing. Since she's also a Seinfeld (married to Jerry, of course), I paired her with a song from Wale's *The Mixtape About Nothing*. Wale is obsessed with *Seinfeld*. Much of his work has been based around his love for the show, including *The Mixtape About Nothing*. There's a song on there that sits at the intersection between *Seinfeld* and the Roots, "The Roots Song That Wale Is On." Later, Jerry collaborated with Wale on a sequel, *The Album About Nothing*. When Wale approached Jerry, Jerry didn't know who he was, but he asked Jessica, and she explained it to him. She's a huge music fan; I know she'll appreciate this choice. Sourcing.

What can you say about cauliflower? When you roast it properly, when you season it inventively, it's delicious. Jessica does both of those things. You should encourage your guests to pull the florets from the core: fewer utensils use means less waste. Also, gluten-free!

For the Cauliflower:
- 3 small heads cauliflower
- 6 tablespoons (90 ml) extra-virgin olive oil
- 2 teaspoons kosher salt
- ¼ teaspoon freshly ground black pepper
- 1½ cups (360 ml) water

For the Smoky Red Pepper Sauce:
- 2 red bell peppers, chopped
- 1 medium beefsteak tomato, cored and seeded
- ½ cup (50 g) grated Parmesan cheese
- ½ cup (70 g) roasted salted almonds
- ¾ teaspoon smoked paprika
- ¼ teaspoon cayenne pepper
- ½ teaspoon kosher salt
- 2 tablespoons extra-virgin olive oil

- 1 tablespoon sherry vinegar or red wine vinegar

For the Spicy Green Sauce:
- 6 jalapeño peppers, seeded and chopped
- 2 scallions, cut into 1-inch (2.5 cm) pieces
- 1 clove garlic, peeled
- 1 bunch cilantro, picked (about 2 cups/32 g)
- 1 large bunch basil, picked (about 3 cups/48 g)
- ½ cup (128 g) mayonnaise
- 2 tablespoons fresh lime juice
- ½ teaspoon kosher salt
- 1 cup (240 ml) sour cream
- A few sprigs of parsley and cilantro, leaves picked, chopped

To make the cauliflower: Preheat the oven to 400°F (205°C). Trim the core from the cauliflower so the heads are able to sit flat in a large roasting pan or baking dish. Turn all three cauliflower upside down and drizzle with 3 tablespoons of the oil (a tablespoon each). Season with 1 teaspoon of salt. Turn the cauliflower over and drizzle with the remaining 3 tablespoons oil, 1 teaspoon salt, and the pepper. Measure the water into the baking dish, then roast for 1 hour, or until golden brown. While the cauliflower is roasting, make the sauces.

To make the red pepper sauce: Combine all the ingredients in a food processor and process until creamy and smooth.

To make the spicy green sauce: Combine all the ingredients except the sour cream in a food processor and process until creamy and smooth. Transfer to a serving bowl and stir in the sour cream. Chill until the cauliflower is ready.

To serve: Top the cauliflower with parsley and cilantro and serve with the sauces.

JONEZ

A lot of people demonize carbs. It's one of the
myths of contemporary society. Carbs get written off as shallow, as immediate gratification,
as empty calories. But through the chefs that
have cooked at my food salons, I have learned
that carbs, done right, can be just as healthy and
sophisticated as any other food group. Pasta,
bread, rice: they are a language all their own,
and it's worth learning to invite some native
speakers to your potluck.

Serves: 6 to 8
Prep time: 15 minutes
Cook time: 25 minutes

Kale Walnut Pesto Pasta
Ashley Graham

Ashley is from Lincoln, Nebraska, which meant that I had to send her Zager and Evans's "In the Year 2525." Most people know this song, even if they don't know that they know it. It's a spacy, even eerie pop oddity from 1969 that imagines the future of human civilization in the then-distant future. The year 2525 is just the starting point: the song rockets ahead to 3535, 4545, and so on, all the way to 9595. It's a strange dystopian song, but I sent it to her because Zager and Evans—even though they sound like a law firm—were two guys from Nebraska who met at college in Lincoln.

I was thinking futuristic, but Ashley defeated me with delicious traditionalism. Pasta, kale, health: her dish was a light source, both in the sense that it was light and that it illuminated the entire potluck. And if you don't like (or don't have) kale, you can substitute other greens like spinach or chard. Just make sure you have the full 10 cups (about 210 g).

- ½ cup (50 g) walnuts
- 1 teaspoon salt, plus more for salting the pasta water
- 1 bunch kale
- 4 ounces (113 g) pecorino cheese, grated
- 1 clove garlic, peeled
- ½ teaspoon salt
- ½ cup (120 ml) olive oil
- 1 pound (454 g) penne, fusilli, or other short pasta

Preheat the oven to 350°F (175°C).

Spread the walnuts on a baking sheet in an even layer. Toast for 6 to 8 minutes, until fragrant and lightly browned. Set aside to cool.

Meanwhile, bring a pot of water to a boil and salt it generously. Strip the leaves from the kale (you should have about 10 cups/210 g) and discard the stems (or save for another use). Blanch the kale just until bright green, then remove with tongs or a slotted spoon and place in a food processor. Don't worry if the kale is still a little wet—the water will help to process the sauce. Reserve the water.

Chop 1 tablespoon of the toasted walnuts and set aside. Add the rest to the food processor with the kale. Add 3½ ounces (100 g) of the cheese, the garlic, and the salt and process, streaming in the oil until everything is finely chopped and incorporated.

Return the pot of water to a boil and cook the pasta according to package instructions. Drain.

Turn the pesto out into a large bowl. When pasta is done, use a slotted spoon to remove the pasta from the water and toss gently with the sauce. Check the seasoning.

Plate the pasta in a serving bowl or platter. Finish with the toasted walnuts and the remaining cheese.

Nastassia's Baked Pasta Frittata

Mark Ladner

Serves: 10 to 12
Prep time: 15 minutes
Cook time: 1 hour

Mark didn't make lasagna, but he made a pasta frittata that wasn't far off. The dish he made was hot out of the oven, but it can also be served at room temperature, which gives it a great afterlife as breakfast leftovers.

For the Garlic Fried Breadcrumbs:
– 1 baguette or small Italian roll
– ¼ cup (120 ml) olive oil
– 3 cloves garlic, smashed
– ½ teaspoon salt

For the Frittata:
– 1 tablespoon softened unsalted
   butter, for the pan
– 2 teaspoons salt, plus more
   for the pasta water
– 1 pound (454 g) spaghetti,
   preferably grano duro
– 6 ounces (170 g) dried Italian
   salami, cut into small dice
– ⅔ cup (53 g) grated Parmesan
   cheese
– ⅓ cup (38 g) shredded
   mozzarella cheese
– 12 large eggs
– 8 ounces (227 g) cherry
   tomatoes, quartered
– 6 zucchini blossoms or
   2 small zucchinis

Mark Ladner is a pasta expert. I like to think of myself a hip-hop expert. Expertise, intersect! There are many songs that reference pasta in one form or another: Chance the Rapper's "I Am Very Very Lonely" and Raekwon's "Ice Water." But really, there's only one that demands to be sent as a creative prompt, and that would be Lil Wayne's "6 Foot 7 Foot," which contains the immortal lyric "Real Gs move in silence like lasagna."

(recipe continues on following page)

Preheat the oven to 250°F (120°C).

To make the garlic fried breadcrumbs: Tear the bread into bite-size pieces and spread them on a baking sheet in a single layer. Bake until crisp and just beginning to turn light golden, about 30 minutes.

Remove the bread from the oven and increase the oven temperature to 400°F (200°C). Let the bread cool for 10 minutes. Using a coffee mug or bottom of a small skillet, smash the bread pieces until they resemble rustic breadcrumbs.

Heat the oil in a large skillet over medium heat until shimmering. Add the garlic and stir for about 30 seconds, until it turns light golden brown. Add the breadcrumbs and cook for another 3 minutes, or until golden brown. Remove the breadcrumbs from the pan to a paper towel–lined plate. When cool enough to handle, toss with a sprinkling of salt.

To make the frittata: Grease a 9 by 13-inch (23 by 33-cm) baking dish with butter.

Bring a large pot of salted water to a boil. Add the spaghetti and cook for 7 minutes. Drain and rinse under cold water until cooled to room temperature. Spread the drained spaghetti in the bottom of the prepared baking dish, then top with the salami and cheeses.

In a large bowl, combine the eggs, 2 teaspoons salt, and ¼ cup (60 ml) water and whisk until frothy. Pour the egg mixture over the spaghetti, making sure it is evenly distributed.

Evenly distribute the quartered tomatoes and garlic fried breadcrumbs over the top. Bake for 12 minutes and check to see if the egg is cooked by giving the pan a shake. If it's not, return it to the oven and check every 5 minutes until the egg is no longer runny.

While the frittata is baking, prepare the zucchini blossoms or zucchini. If using blossoms, gently pick the flowers from the stems, keeping them in one piece if possible. If using zucchini, with a sharp knife or mandoline, gently slice the zucchini lengthwise into ⅛-inch (3-mm) strips.

Remove the frittata from the oven and immediately lay the blossoms or zucchini over the top. Let rest for 15 minutes before serving.

Tuna Pasta à la Popowendy

Humberto Leon

Serves: 8 to 10
Prep time: 10 minutes
Cook time: 15 minutes

Tuna pasta is the OG of a "bring it over" dish. We all have a tuna pasta story, right? But when you serve that tuna pasta in a Russel Wright pink bowl with wooden serving utensils, the whole thing gets kicked up a notch.

- 1 teaspoon salt, plus more for the pasta water
- Splash of olive oil
- 1 pound (454 g) pasta, such as penne or rigatoni
- ¾ cup (75 g) frozen peas
- ¼ red onion, finely diced
- 2 (5-ounce/142-g) cans wild-caught tuna in water
- 5 tablespoons (73 g) mayonnaise
- 1 teaspoon garlic powder
- Freshly ground black pepper

Bring a large pot of water to a boil, salt it, and add the oil. Add the pasta and cook at a rolling boil for 7 minutes.

While the pasta is cooking, soak the peas in warm water. Drain the peas, add them to the pasta water, and cook for 30 seconds. Drain the peas and pasta into a colander and quickly rinse with cold water. Place in a large bowl and, while warm, toss with the onion.

Add the tuna, mayonnaise, garlic powder, a few cracks of black pepper, and the salt. Toss gently and serve.

When I first met Humberto and Carol Lim—his partner in Open Ceremony and Kenzo—it struck me that the international mix that they have to contend with every day is intense. They came from New York roots to oversee a Parisian label founded by a Japanese designer. I picked a song from Pizzicato Five, which has the same sense of internationalism, adventure, and fun. The song, "Past, Present, Future," is partly about the way that pleasure works against the passage of time. Great food has the same effect.

Serves: 8 to 10
Prep time: 10 minutes
Cook time: 40 minutes

Old Dirty Basmati Rice
Tanya Holland

Tanya Holland has been a huge influence on me without even knowing it; her cookbook *New Soul Cooking* taught me so much about soul food and the ways that it reflects both promises and the problems in African American history. She's also a central figure in the Oakland cultural scene, which means that she gets one of the monuments of Oakland soul, Tony! Toni! Toné!'s "Let's Get Down." It's a party song. Food can be a party.

A hot skillet, delicious rice, vegetables scattered throughout for flavor and texture . . . is there anything that communicates the idea of community more effectively? I knew Tanya's rice would taste great before I tried it. I was also told, in confidence, that if you don't have time to make the Creole spice, store-bought spice isn't a total loss.

For the Creole Spice:
- 1 teaspoon cayenne pepper
- ½ teaspoon freshly ground black pepper
- ½ teaspoon paprika
- 2 tablespoons salt
- 2 tablespoons herbes de Provence
- 2 tablespoons ground cumin

For the Rice:
- 1½ cups (278 g) basmati rice
- 3 cups (720 ml) water
- 2 bay leaves
- 1 teaspoon kosher salt
- 2 tablespoons olive oil
- 8 ounces (227 g) chicken livers, chopped
- 1 pound (454 g) pork sausage (if using links, remove the casing)
- 3 green onions, thinly sliced, whites and greens separated
- 1 green bell pepper, diced
- 1 red bell pepper, diced
- 1 jalapeño pepper, finely diced, seeds removed if desired
- 2 cloves garlic, minced
- 1 tablespoon Creole Spice

- 1 cup (240 ml) chicken stock
- ¼ cup (60 ml) Worcestershire sauce
- 2 tablespoons tamari or soy sauce
- 5 thyme sprigs, leaves picked and chopped
- 5 sprigs fresh parsley, leaves picked and chopped
- 2 cups (40 g) baby spinach
- Your favorite hot sauce

To make the Creole spice: In a small jar, combine all of the ingredients. Will keep for 3 to 6 months.

To make the rice: Place the rice in a fine-mesh sieve over a large bowl of cold water. Rinse the rice, changing the water up to 5 times, until the water runs clear. Shake off the excess water from the rice and add the rice to a medium pot with a tight-fitting lid. Add the water, the bay leaves, and the salt and bring to a boil over medium-high heat. Turn the burner down to the lowest setting, cover, and cook for 18 minutes. Remove the pot from the heat and let sit, covered, for 10 minutes.

Heat the oil in a large skillet over medium-high heat. Add the chicken livers and cook just until no longer pink and browned on the edges, 4 to 6 minutes. Remove with a slotted spoon to a bowl and set aside. Repeat this step with the sausage, breaking it up as it begins to brown.

Turn the heat down to medium and add the white parts of the green onions, the bell peppers, and jalapeño and cook until the vegetables begin to soften, 4 to 6 minutes. Add the garlic and Creole spice and cook for 30 seconds.

Add the livers, sausage, rice, stock, Worcestershire sauce, and tamari. Stir to coat the rice, decrease the heat to low, and cook for an additional 15 minutes until everything is coated and the flavors have melded.

Add the thyme, the green parts of the green onions, the parsley, and spinach and cook just until wilted. Serve immediately, with hot sauce.

JOLLOF WARS

I remember Kwame Onwuachi telling me about jollof rice when I ate at his restaurant in D.C. It's basically a rice-and-tomato-based pot that gets customized to suit the vision of a particular cook. It's a dish of the people, literally: the name comes from the Wolofs of West Africa. Jollof wars are a big deal in the Nigerian diaspora. People bring their unbeatable family recipes and pit them against other people's unbeatable family recipes. There's even a big competition in D.C. to judge the best jollof. The Young Senators would be proud. But the great jollof-off also reminded me that potlucks are about collaboration and also, beneath that, sometimes about competition, and that put me in the mind of "Blame It on the Boogie." It's a famous hit by the Jacksons, from the 1978 album *Destiny*; it was the first album I bought when I came off a major punishment in 1978. "Blame It on the Boogie" was a Jackson original, but it wasn't. It was written by a British songwriter named Mick Jackson. He had recorded his own original version, and British radio stations pitted them against each other in a battle of the boogie. I dedicate "Blame It on the Boogie" not to Kwame alone, not to Yvonne Orji alone, but to both of them, and to the jollof wars.

Jollof Rice with Jerk Chicken and Marinated Gooseberries
Kwame Onwuachi

Serves: 8 to 10
Prep time: 20 minutes
Cook time: 45 minutes

Everything about this dish radiates heat: the colors are hot colors, the food is hot food, and the enthusiasm that it sparked in potluck guests was off the charts. That's what jollof does!

For the Red Sauce:
- 3 red bell peppers, chopped
- 3 large tomatoes, chopped
- ½ cup (128 g) tomato paste
- 1 large red onion
- 1 (2-inch/5-cm) piece fresh ginger
- 3 cloves garlic, peeled
- 1 Maggi seasoning cube
- 2 tablespoons habanero hot sauce
- 2 tablespoons curry powder
- 2 teaspoons salt
- 3 tablespoons canola oil

For the Jerk Paste and Chicken:
- ½ cup (120 ml) soy sauce
- 1 bunch green onions, whites chopped, greens reserved for garnish
- 2 habanero peppers, seeded if desired, chopped
- 2 tablespoons tamarind paste
- Leaves from 5 thyme sprigs
- ⅓ cup (83 ml) Worcestershire sauce
- 1 (2-inch/5-cm) piece fresh ginger, roughly chopped
- 2 cloves garlic, peeled
- ¼ cup (50 g) sugar
- 2 tablespoons salt
- ½ teaspoon ground allspice
- 1 teaspoon ground cinnamon
- 2 bay leaves
- ½ teaspoon ground cloves
- Canola oil, for greasing the grill
- 1 chicken (3 to 4 pounds/1.3 to 1.8 kg), cut into 8 pieces

For the Jollof Rice:
- 3 tablespoons canola oil
- 1½ cups (237 g) basmati rice
- 1 habanero pepper, diced
- 1 cup (240 ml) red sauce
- 3 cups water
- 1 teaspoon salt

For the Gooseberries:
- 2 limes, juiced
- 1 tablespoon honey
- 1 tablespoon olive oil
- ½ teaspoon kosher salt
- 1 pint (340 g) gooseberries, halved

For Serving:
- Reserved scallion greens
- Chopped fresh parsley

Kwame has taken pains to be an ambassador for Afro-Caribbean cooking—whenever I'm at one of his restaurants, he comes out and tells us about the ingredients, the preparations, and even the palette (once he made sorbets shaped like hot peppers, and he talked about the impact of reds, yellows, and oranges in a dessert setting). That was in D.C., which led me to go-go music: go-go, of course, is the capital's brand of homegrown funk, which stretched into the early days of hip-hop and combined and recombined its DNA. I went for the Young Senators, a first-wave D.C. group, and picked "Jungle," their best-known song. It was released on the band's own label, Innovation Records. The name resonates. The independence resonates. The ambition resonates.

(recipe continues on following page)

To make the red sauce: In a blender, combine all the ingredients except the oil and blend until smooth.

In a heavy-bottomed pot, heat the oil over medium heat. Add the contents of the blender, bring to a simmer, then reduce the heat to low and cook until the water from the tomatoes has cooked out of the sauce, about 10 minutes. Set aside.

To make the jerk paste and marinate the chicken: In a blender, combine all the ingredients except the chicken and blend until smooth. Place the chicken and jerk sauce in a zip-top bag or bowl and coat each piece of chicken well.

To make the rice: Heat the oil in a large pot with a tight-fitting lid over medium heat. Add the rice and toast it for about 2 to 4 minutes, stirring frequently. Add the habanero and cook for another 2 minutes.

Add the red sauce and salt and cook for 2 more minutes. Add the water and salt and stir to combine. Bring to a boil, then decrease the heat to maintain a simmer. Cover and cook for 18 minutes. Remove from the heat and let the rice steam, covered, for 10 minutes.

To cook the chicken: Set a grill to medium heat or heat a grill pan over medium heat. Remove the chicken from the marinade and oil the grill well. Grill the chicken, turning every few minutes, for 15 to 20 minutes, until the pieces reach an internal temperature of 165°F (75°C). Remove from the grill to a plate.

To make the gooseberries: In a small bowl, whisk together the lime juice, honey, oil, and salt. Add the gooseberries and mix gently to coat.

To serve: Fluff the rice and spoon it onto a large serving platter. Place the chicken on top of the rice, spoon the gooseberries over everything, and finish with the scallion greens and chopped parsley.

Coconut Jollof Rice
Yvonne Orji

Serves: 10 to 12
Prep time: 20 minutes
Cook time: 35 minutes

What's great about a jollof dish is that there are no rules. Yvonne's version can easily be made vegetarian by removing the shrimp.

- 4 cups (720 g) long-grain white rice, such as basmati or jasmine
- ½ cup (120 ml) olive oil
- 2 large beefsteak tomatoes, diced
- 1 red onion, diced
- 2 habanero peppers, diced
- 2 tablespoons salt
- 2 tablespoons curry powder
- 1 teaspoon smoked paprika
- 1 tablespoon dried thyme
- 1 teaspoon dried basil
- 1 teaspoon freshly ground black pepper
- 1 (14-ounce/400-ml) can coconut milk
- 2 Maggi seasoning cubes
- 1 pound (454 g) jumbo shrimp, peeled
- Unsweetened toasted coconut flakes (optional)

Yvonne is Nigerian American, which put me in mind of Fela Kuti, and the subject of this book put me in mind of Fela's song "Water No Get Enemy." In part it's because the song's lyrics talk about the universality of water; one of the lines is (I'm paraphrasing from the Pidgin) "If you want to make soup, you have to use water." It was also because there are competing versions of that song. There's the Fela original, which came out in 1975, and then there's the remix we made for *Red, Hot, and Fela* in 2013, which featured D'Angelo, Macy Gray, Nile Rodgers, Roy Hargrove, and others.

(recipe continues on following page)

Wash the rice until the water runs clear. Bring a large pot of water to a boil and add the rice. Cook it like pasta for 10 minutes, then drain the rice into a sieve and rinse it once more.

Heat the oil in a Dutch oven or other heavy-bottomed large pot over medium heat. Add the tomatoes, onion, and habaneros and cook until golden brown, 6 to 8 minutes. Add the salt, curry powder, and paprika and cook to meld the flavors for 3 minutes. Add the thyme, basil, and pepper and stir to combine.

Stir in the parboiled rice, coconut milk, Maggi cubes, and enough water just to cover the rice. Bring to a boil, then lower the heat to maintain a simmer, partially cover, and cook for 10 minutes. Add the shrimp, cover fully, and cook for 5 minutes more until bright pink and plump.

Remove the cover and give the rice a final toss. Serve with toasted coconut flakes, if using, for added crunch.

Yvonne's tip:
Follow the first step closely, making sure you rinse the rice! This helps to keep the grains separate, which is what makes jollof rice special.

MEAT

EATERS

At restaurants, main courses and entrees are the names above the title. At potlucks, they're part of an ensemble cast—as I've said before, the host just doesn't have enough control over time and space, when people arrive, where they're sitting, and what size plate sits comfortably on the table in front of them. But entrees and mains are still one of the places where cooks do some of their most substantive work.

Serves: 10
Prep time: 30 minutes
Cook time: 15 minutes

Air-Fried Chicken Burgers
Jimmy Fallon

One of my favorite Jimmy musical impressions is when he does Bruce Springsteen. Some people say his Neil Young is his best, but I have a soft spot for his Bruce—I came to Springsteen's music relatively late, and the things I thought about it as I was learning it are the same things that I sense in Jimmy's imitation. I wanted to find a Springsteen song about food, but I had some trouble. I'll admit that I don't know every lyric and every bootleg. I went for "Hungry Heart," which amused me when I heard it on the radio as a kid, because I saw it in my mind as a *School-house Rock*–style cartoon, with an actual heart chowing down on burgers and fries at the boardwalk. (I also thought that Baltimore Jack was the name of the main character. That one I'm going to keep believing for a while.)

Jimmy really is a burger aficionado. During his travels he always seeks out the best burger and has even had guests on *The Tonight Show* eat burgers with him. So I'm telling you, when Jimmy makes a burger, it's gonna be damn good. This time he is mixing it up with chicken. He's using a countertop air fryer, mostly because he has one and is always trying to find some use for it.

- 2 packs Martin's Potato Rolls (16 rolls)
- 2 pounds (907 g) ground chicken breast
- 1 cup (240 ml) milk
- 1 cup (125 g) diced white onion
- 1 jalapeño pepper, diced
- ½ teaspoon cayenne pepper
- 2 teaspoons salt
- 1½ teaspoons freshly ground black pepper
- 1 cup (46 g) Italian breadcrumbs
- Olive oil cooking spray
- 10 slices Kraft American Cheese Singles
- 1 head green leaf lettuce, leaves separated
- 2 to 3 beefsteak tomatoes, sliced (to make 10 slices)
- Sriracha

Preheat an air fryer. Tear the buns into large pieces and use a food processor to pulse 6 of the buns, working a few at a time, so the bread crumbles and doesn't become mushy.

In a large bowl, combine the ground chicken, milk, onion, jalapeño, cayenne, salt, and pepper. Add half of the crumbled buns from the food processor and ½ cup (23 g) breadcrumbs.

Set aside the remaining half of the crumbled buns and the remaining ½ cup (23 g) of the breadcrumbs on a plate.

Using your hands, mix well to incorporate all the ingredients.

Divide the mixture in half, then divide each half into 5 equal portions. Form 5 burger patties with each half to make 10 bun-size, ½-inch (1.2-cm)-thick patties. Coat all sides of the patties with the reserved breadcrumb mixture, then spray each with the cooking spray.

Place as many burgers as will fit in the air fryer, close it, and cook for 4 minutes. Flip and cook for an additional 4 minutes. Add the cheese and cook for about 30 seconds, until the cheese is melted.

While the burgers are cooking, toast the remaining buns in the toaster, or a toaster oven. Lay out the lettuce, tomato, and sriracha and gather your guests to assemble their burgers.

Serves: 8 to 10
Prep time: 20 minutes,
plus overnight marinating
Cook time: 25 minutes

Heidi's Million Dollar Chicken
Carol Lim

Carol told me once that she had a great chicken recipe. I wasn't sure that was what she would send in for the book, but I thought it was at least a possibility. That led my mind right to Rufus Thomas and the Stax dance classic "Do the Funky Chicken." But I didn't stop there. I went right on through to the "Funky Robot," the "Funky Bird," the "Funky Mississippi," and wound up at the best one of all: "Do the Funky Penguin," one of the slipperiest and slickest achievements in the history of Memphis funk. It's been sampled by Busta Rhymes and Ghostface Killah—and now, by me, right here.

Korean fried chicken is so universally loved because it's double fried. You gotta achieve that crunch. That's what makes this recipe, which comes from from Carol's mom, Heidi, the perfect potluck dish. That crunch is gonna stick. Carol suggests serving your million-dollar chicken on a Yi Yoon Shin celadon plate along with a Korean beer.

For the Chicken Wings:
– 2 teaspoons salt
– Freshly ground black pepper
– 1 quart (950 ml) buttermilk
– 2 pounds (907 g) chicken wings, split into drumettes and flats
– 1 quart vegetable oil
– 3 cups Beksul Korean frying mix, or panko

For the Sauce:
– ½ cup (120 ml) soy sauce
– 1 tablespoon gochujang
– 1 tablespoon brown sugar
– 2 teaspoons toasted sesame oil
– 1 tablespoon rice vinegar
– 2 tablespoons canola oil
– 3 cloves garlic, thinly sliced

For Serving:
– 4 scallions, thinly sliced
– 2 tablespoons toasted sesame seeds
– Steamed white rice (optional)

To make the chicken wings: In a large bowl or container, whisk the salt and about 15 twists of the peppermill into the buttermilk. Add the chicken wings, toss to coat, cover, and place in the fridge overnight to tenderize.

Pour oil into a Dutch oven or other wide, high-sided large pot to a depth of 1½ inches (4 cm) and heat over medium heat until a fry thermometer reaches reaches 350°F (175°C) or when a bit of the frying mix dropped into the oil floats and turns golden brown.

Remove the wings from the buttermilk and place on a wire rack set into a baking sheet to let the brine drip off.

Pour the frying mix into a shallow bowl. Dredge the wings in the mix a few at a time and place them back on the wire rack.

Working in batches, add the wings to the oil, being careful not to overcrowd the pot. Fry for 7 to 10 minutes, until light golden brown. When the wings are done, place them on a clean wire rack or a paper towel–lined plate.

To make the sauce: In a small bowl, whisk the soy sauce, gochujang, brown sugar, toasted sesame oil, and vinegar.

In a large skillet, heat the oil over medium heat. Add the garlic and cook until light golden brown, about 1 minute.

Add the sauce and cook until the brown sugar is dissolved and the sauce begins to look sticky, about 1 minute. Add the wings and toss to coat. Add the scallions and sesame seeds. Serve with rice on the side, if desired.

Carol's tip: My mother uses chicken breast, but it can be swapped out for any cut of chicken.

Thịt Kho Tàu
(Vietnamese Braised Pork Belly)
Kevin Tien

Serves: 8 to 10
Prep time: 20 minutes,
plus at least 1 hour marinating
Cook time: 2 hours and 20 minutes

Kevin's dish delivered more flavor per square inch than I could have possibly expected. It comes in a big pot, so make sure that when you serve this at your potluck you have plenty of small bowls around. This recipe is also a great place to start learning to make caramel sauce.

- 1½ pounds (680 g) pork belly,
  cut into 1-inch (2.5-cm) cubes
- 2 tablespoons fish sauce
- 1 teaspoon freshly ground
  black pepper
- 6 large eggs
- 1 cup (200 g) sugar
- ¼ cup (60 ml) water
- 2 shallots, minced
- 3 Thai chiles,
  sliced into thin rings
- 1 (12-ounce/355-ml) can
  Coco Rico soda
- 1 bunch scallions, thinly sliced
- Steamed white rice, for serving

Kevin's cooking combines his Vietnamese heritage and his Louisiana roots. I don't know if there's a word yet for that kind of fusion. But I do remember recently reading about the Vietnamese community in New Orleans, in Village de l'Est. That got me thinking about directions, and that got me thinking about Fats Domino's "Let the Four Winds Blow," where they blow from the east to the west, just like Kevin's cooking.

(recipe continues on following page)

Toss the pork belly with the fish sauce and pepper and let it marinate in the refrigerator for at least 1 hour or up to overnight.

When the pork is nearly finished marinating, bring a medium pot of water to a boil. Gently place the eggs into the boiling water and boil for 6 minutes (make sure to use a timer). While the eggs are boiling, prepare an ice bath. When the timer goes off, use a slotted spoon to remove the eggs from the boiling water and drop them into the ice bath. This will ensure that they peel easy. Once the eggs have cooled, peel them and set aside.

In a Dutch oven or other heavy-bottomed large pot, combine the sugar and water and stir over medium-low heat until the sugar dissolves. Leave the mixture alone without stirring for 5 to 6 minutes to create a caramel, watching closely as the color changes from light golden to a rich amber color. Once this color is reached, immediately remove the pot from the heat.

Add the shallots and Thai chiles and leave to cook from the residual heat of the caramel until slightly softened and aromatic, about 2 minutes. Return the pot to medium heat, add the pork belly, and toss it in the caramel sauce to evenly coat.

Stir in the soda, increase the heat to high, and bring to a boil. Lower the heat to maintain a simmer, partially cover, and simmer for about 2 hours, until the pork belly is very tender. Remove the pot from the heat and skim the fat from the top if needed. Place the soft-boiled eggs into the sauce to stain them a caramel color and infuse them with the flavor of the pork.

Top with the scallions and serve with steamed white rice.

Lamb Chops with Mint Salsa over Couscous
Athena Calderone

Serves: 8
Prep time: 20 minutes
Cook time: 20 minutes

The smell of this dish got me even before the taste. It hit from maybe six feet away, and it was incredible. And the salsa is so good that people may want to use it on other dishes. Go ahead. It's a potluck. Dishes talking to each other is part of the fun.

For the Mint Salsa Verde:
– 1½ cups (45 g) mint leaves
– ¾ cup (23 g) fresh parsley leaves
– 2 cloves garlic, finely chopped
– 1 small shallot, finely diced
– 1 habanero pepper, finely chopped
– ¾ cup (180 ml) extra-virgin olive oil
– ¼ cup (60 ml) fresh lemon juice
– 1 teaspoon salt,
  plus more to taste
– Freshly ground black pepper

For the Currant Couscous:
– ⅓ cup (75 ml) vinegar
– 3 tablespoons currants
– 2 teaspoons extra-virgin olive oil
– ½ yellow onion, finely diced
– 1 clove garlic, finely chopped
– 1 teaspoon cumin seeds,
  lightly crushed
– 1½ cups (360 ml) chicken stock
– 1 cup (195 g) couscous
– ¼ cup (35 g) pine nuts, toasted
– 1 teaspoon salt, plus more to taste
– Freshly ground black pepper

For the Lamb Chops:
– 1 teaspoon black peppercorns,
  crushed
– 2½ teaspoons cumin seeds
– 2½ teaspoons coriander seeds
– 2 teaspoons salt, plus more
  to taste
– 8 bone-in lamb rib chops

"Moonshadow" by Cat Stevens isn't about food. I'm not sure what it's about. Moons? Shadows? What's strange about this song is that before I heard the original, I heard a cover version by Patti LaBelle. It's an epically long cover version, close to ten minutes, and halfway through, Patti begins to monologue about various things, including cooking and soul food. Patti makes it her own. Much cooking is sort of a version of this process—not purely original composition so much as creating distinctive cover versions. Athena won't be the first person to cook whatever she cooks, but she can put her stamp on it.

(recipe continues on following page)

To make the salsa verde: Finely chop the mint and parsley. Transfer to a bowl and add the garlic, shallot, ¼ teaspoon of the diced habanero, the oil, lemon juice, salt, and pepper to taste. Taste and add more habanero, if desired, or set aside for guests to help themselves if they want a bit more heat.

To make the couscous: In a small saucepan, heat the vinegar over low heat until steaming. Remove from the heat and add the currants.

Heat the oil in a saucepan with a tight-fitting lid over medium heat. Add the onion and garlic and cook for 3 to 5 minutes, until translucent and barely golden. Add the cumin and cook until fragrant, about 1 minute. Add the chicken stock and bring the mixture to a boil.

Stir in the couscous, cover the pan, and remove from the heat. Let sit for 10 minutes, then remove the lid and gently fluff with a fork. Drain the currants and fold them into the couscous along with the toasted pine nuts. Add the salt and season with pepper.

To make the lamb chops: While the couscous is sitting, preheat a grill pan or outdoor grill over medium-high heat to about 400°F (200°C).

Combine the crushed peppercorns, cumin, coriander, and salt in a small bowl. Season the lamb evenly with the spice mixture.

Grill the chops for about 3 minutes on each side, until lightly charred. Tent with foil and let rest for 10 minutes.

To serve: Spoon the couscous onto a serving platter, top with the lamb, and spoon the salsa verde over the top. Serve the remaining salsa verde in a small dish on the side for people to help themselves.

Spicy Sweet and Sour Chicken with Lemongrass

Andrew Zimmern

Serves: 10 to 14
Prep time: 20 minutes
Cook time: 1 hour

Someone once told me that even in dishes with strong sauces, the taste of the sauce should not overpower the meat, but rather complement it. I don't remember exactly who that was, but that person was absolutely correct, and Andrew's dish proves it. Plus, there is something special about the way he prepares the rice. Follow his instructions.

– 5 dried árbol chiles, split lengthwise, seeds removed
– 3 fresh Thai chiles, chopped
– 4 lemongrass stalks, tender inner part only, chopped
– 8 shallots, diced
– 8 cloves garlic, diced
– 1 tablespoon ground turmeric
– 1½ teaspoons ground cinnamon
– 1 tablespoon salt, plus more to taste
– 10 medium skinless, boneless chicken thighs
– 3 tablespoons peanut oil or other neutral oil
– 1 cup (240 ml) ketchup
– ½ cup (120 ml) white distilled or rice vinegar
– ¼ cup (50 g) sugar
– ½ cup (120 ml) water
– 3 carrots, diced
– 1½ cups (218 g) peas, defrosted if frozen
– ½ cup (15 g) fresh mint leaves
– Steamed white rice, for serving

Andrew writes about the far corners of the world and what food does in those places. I wanted to think of a song that was both exotic and earthy, one that traveled far and wide without losing its footing. One of the songs that I have always kept close to my heart is Rufus's "Egyptian Song," the final song on the 1977 album *Ask Rufus*. I have my own set of memories around that song: it's what was playing when my parents told me that they were going away on tour. Later on I discovered that there was a Prefect of Egypt named Rufus in the first century. Anyway, this is the song that stuck in my mind when I considered Andrew, because it harmonizes with themes of travel and home, of the Midwest and the Middle East.

(recipe continues on following page)

In a small pot, bring 1 cup (240 ml) water to a boil. Remove from the heat, add the árbol chiles, and set aside to soak for 20 to 30 minutes until softened. Drain.

In a food processor, combine the árbol chiles and Thai chiles, lemongrass, shallots, and garlic and process until a paste forms.

In a large bowl, combine the turmeric, cinnamon, and the salt. Then add the chicken to the bowl and toss in the spice mixture.

Heat the oil in a large cast-iron skillet over medium-high heat until shimmering. Working in batches and being careful not to crowd the pan, add the chicken thighs and cook until golden brown, about 5 minutes on each side. Transfer to a plate.

Decrease the heat to medium, add the chile-shallot paste to the skillet, and cook, stirring, until golden brown, about 5 minutes.

Add the ketchup, vinegar, sugar, and the water and bring to a simmer. Return the chicken to the skillet and simmer for 10 minutes. Add the carrots and cook for 5 minutes, then add the peas and cook for an additional 5 minutes, or until the chicken is tender and fully cooked.

Fold in most of the mint leaves and check the seasonings. Transfer the chicken and sauce to a serving platter and top with remaining mint leaves. Serve with white rice.

JJ's Sticky Ribs

J. J. Johnson

Serves: 12 to 15
Prep time: 10 minutes,
plus 5 hours marinating
Cook time: 2 hours and 15 minutes

Ribs are mostly about two things—taste and texture—and this recipe gets them both right.

For the Ribs:
– 2 racks pork baby back ribs
  (3 pounds/1.3 kg each)
– 1¾ cups (434 ml) Thai sweet chili sauce
– ¾ cup (180 ml) soy sauce
– 2 tablespoons green curry paste
– 2 teaspoons fish sauce
– 2 tablespoons grated,
  peeled fresh ginger
– 2 cloves garlic, grated

For the Sauce:
– ⅓ cup (85 g) all-natural smooth
  peanut butter, melted
– ½ cup (120 ml) soy sauce
– 3 tablespoons tomato paste
– ¼ cup (60 ml) water
– 3 tablespoons light brown sugar
– ¼ cup (60 ml) Thai sweet chili sauce
– 2 tablespoons rice vinegar
– 2 teaspoons Thai green curry paste
– 1½ tablespoons smoked paprika
– ¼ cup Thai basil leaves, torn

For Serving:
– 3 sprigs Thai basil
– Roasted salted peanuts

Back in 2017, I was honored to have J. J. come to one of my food salons and cook for me there. That night, he spoke about how his Puerto Rican grandmother, who was in charge of the family kitchen when he was growing up, instilled in him the idea that food is inherently a form of grandmothering: of extending care and protection and even fierce love to those around you. That concept remained central to his sense of a restaurant's mission and its responsibility; he explained that restaurants have to be serious about fighting problems like hunger and poverty in the communities that surround and nurture them. As luck would have it, J. J. shares a name with J. J. Johnson, the great jazz trombonist, a pioneer of bebop. Both Johnsons have shown a respect for history and also a willingness to disrupt it in the name of creativity. I chose "100 Proof," from the 1957 album *Blue Trombone*, which demonstrates how to highlight technique and innovation at the same time. As jazz guys liked to say, it cooks.

(recipe continues on following page)

To make the ribs: Season the ribs generously with salt. In a medium bowl, mix the chili sauce, soy sauce, green curry paste, fish sauce, ginger, and garlic. Place the ribs in two large zip-top bags or a roasting pan and pour the marinade over the ribs. Seal the bags or cover the pan with foil and place in the refrigerator for 5 hours to marinate. Allow the ribs to come to room temperature before baking.

Preheat the oven to 300°F (150°C).

Place the ribs on a baking sheet and cover tightly with foil. Roast for 1½ to 2 hours, until the meat is easily pierced through with a small knife but not completely falling apart.

To make the sauce: While the ribs are roasting, melt the peanut butter in a small saucepan over medium heat until smooth, then remove from the heat and whisk in the remaining sauce ingredients.

To finish the dish and serve: Remove the foil and spoon the sauce over the ribs. Roast for 10 to 15 minutes more, until the sauce begins to look baked into the ribs. Cut into individual ribs and serve garnished with Thai basil and peanuts.

Serves: 12 to 16
Prep time: 20 minutes
Cook time: 2½ hours

Country Captain Chicken
Mashama Bailey

Mashama has cooked and lived in Georgia—she was nominated for a James Beard Award for her restaurant The Grey, but she's Bronx born, which means that it was nearly impossible for her to avoid early hip-hop. The actual story of hip-hop's birth is twisty and complex, but most people accept the Bronx as the borough of its birth: first through the turntable parties of DJ Kool Herc, then through various other innovators, few as innovative as Afrika Bambaataa. I didn't want to pick "Planet Rock," not because it's not great, but because it's almost too iconic at this point. For Mashama, a better match was "Renegades of Funk," equally great and full of rebellious attitude and a respect for history.

Most people have eaten so much chicken in their lives that they forget how it can be a revelation in the hands of a talented chef. Mashama is one of those chefs. This recipe hits all the notes: savory, sweet, spicy. And you may want to make copies of the recipe, because people will ask you for it.

- 4 tablespoons (56 g) unsalted butter
- 5 tablespoons (75 ml) olive oil
- 2 chickens (3 ½ to 4 pounds/1.6 to 1.8 kg each), cut into 8 pieces
- 2 tablespoons salt, plus more to taste
- Freshly ground black pepper
- 2 large onions, diced
- 4 green bell peppers, diced
- 4 serrano chiles, finely diced
- 1 head garlic, finely chopped
- 2 tablespoons curry powder
- 2 (28-ounce/794-g) cans diced tomatoes, drained
- 3 cups (720 ml) white wine
- 1 quart (950 ml) chicken stock
- ¾ cup (110 g) raisins or currants
- 10 sprigs chopped fresh parsley, for serving

Heat a large Dutch oven or other heavy-bottomed pot over medium heat and add 1 tablespoon butter and 1 tablespoon oil. Season the chicken parts all over with salt and pepper. Working in batches, cook the chicken parts until they are deep golden brown on all sides, 8 to 10 minutes, then remove from the pan and set aside.

Scrape any browned or burned bits from the bottom of the pot and give it a wipe if necessary.

Add the remaining 3 tablespoons butter and 1 tablespoon of the remaining oil to the pot along with the onions, bell peppers, chiles, garlic, and season with salt and pepper. Reduce the heat to low and cook until the vegetables are tender and translucent, 3 to 5 minutes, then stir in the curry powder.

Add the drained tomatoes, increase the heat to medium, and cook until the vegetables begin to caramelize, 8 to 10 minutes. Deglaze the pan with the wine and cook until the wine is reduced by half, about 5 to 8 minutes. Add the stock and bring to a boil.

Add the remaining 3 tablespoons oil along with the browned chicken. Reduce the heat to maintain a simmer and cook for 1 to 1 ½ hours, until the chicken is very tender.

At the last moment, add the currants and season once more. Finish with the parsley and serve.

Braised Osso Bucco
with Fennel Soffritto
Missy Robbins

Serves: 8
Prep time: 20 minutes,
plus 1 to 24 hours marinating
Cook time: 2 hours

Serve this dish alongside your favorite loaf of bread, and if you want, bring roasted potatoes or polenta—that gives you a whole meal.

- 4 center-cut veal shanks, each 2 inches (5 cm) thick (about 14 ounces/397 g each), tied with twine
- Kosher salt
- ½ cup (120 ml) olive oil, divided
- 3 large bulbs fennel, fronds reserved, finely chopped
- 2 large carrots, finely chopped
- 1 large onion, finely chopped
- 4 cloves garlic, thinly sliced
- 1½ cups (360 ml) dry white wine
- 1 (28-ounce/794-g) can whole San Marzano tomatoes, crushed by hand
- 1 tablespoon fennel seeds, ground
- 1½ teaspoons red chile flakes
- 2 sprigs rosemary
- 5 sprigs thyme
- 1 teaspoon fennel pollen, for garnish
- Fennel fronds, for garnish

Generously salt the veal shanks on all sides and set aside in the refrigerator for at least 1 hour and preferably overnight.

Heat a large Dutch oven or other heavy-bottomed pot over medium-high heat with ¼ cup (60 ml) olive oil. Sear the shanks on all sides until browned, 3 to 5 minutes per side. Remove the shanks and set aside on a plate. Scrape any dark bits from the bottom of the Dutch oven and wipe out with a paper towel if needed.

Add the remaining ¼ cup (60 ml) olive oil, fennel, carrots, and onion to the pot. Cook for 3 minutes, then add the garlic and cook for an additional 5 to 8 minutes, stirring regularly, until the vegetables are tender and slightly golden. This is your soffritto. Return the shanks to the pot and add the wine. Cook until the wine is reduced by half, 6 to 8 minutes.

Add the crushed tomatoes, ground fennel seeds, and chile flakes. Add water to cover the shanks by 1 inch (2.5 cm). Bring to a boil, then lower the heat to maintain a low simmer. After 45 minutes add the rosemary and thyme. Cook for 1 to 1½ hours, until the meat is almost falling off the bone. Place the shanks in a serving bowl and ladle the sauce over them. Garnish the dish with fennel pollen and the fennel fronds.

I decided to inspire Missy Robbins with a song by Missy Elliott. Many of her songs are inspirational: "Work It," "Gossip Folks," "WTF." I went for "I'm Better," her chilly, spacy 2017 single. On this song, Missy (Elliott) collaborates with Lamb. This is a good time for me to clear up a misconception. Lamb isn't nicknamed that because of a fondness for Lamborghinis, though he may have it. He's nicknamed that because, well, it's his last name. I expect the same sleek minimalism as this song.

Fried Rabbit
Chris Fischer

Serves: 8 to 10
Prep time: 20 minutes,
plus up to 24 hours brining
Cook time: 40 minutes

Fried rabbit looks like fried chicken, and it tastes a little bit like that, but a little more like rabbit. Chris brined the meat in cider, which is a neat double trick, because it also allowed him to have a glass of cider while cooking.

For the Brine and Rabbit:
- 1 cup (240 ml) buttermilk
- ¼ cup (60 ml) hard cider
- ¼ cup (60 g) plain yogurt
- 1 large egg, beaten
- 1 shallot, roughly chopped
- 2 tablespoons salt
- 2 whole rabbits, each split into 9 parts (ask your butcher)

For the Dry Mix:
- 2 cups (316 g) rice flour
- 1 cup (80 g) panko breadcrumbs
- ⅓ cup (51 g) potato starch
- 1 tablespoon red chile flakes
- 1 tablespoon salt
- 1 tablespoon baking powder
- 2 quarts (2 L) grapeseed oil
- Salt

For Serving:
- Jar of pickles (dealer's choice)
- Small jar of mayonnaise or homemade aioli

In a large bowl, whisk together all of the brine ingredients and add the rabbit. Refrigerate the rabbit for a minimum of 2 hours or in the brine overnight. Remove the rabbit from the refrigerator 90 minutes before frying.

In a shallow bowl, whisk together all of the dry ingredients. Set up your fry station. Place the dry mix as close as possible to the burner. Place the brined rabbit next to that. Set a baking sheet fitted with a wire rack for the finished rabbit on the opposite side of your fry pot.

In a large, high-sided pot or a Dutch oven, heat the oil to between 375 and 425°F (190 to 220°C). If you don't have a fry thermometer, drop a pinch of the dry mix in the oil to assess the heat. It will bubble and float when it's ready.

Remove the rabbit from the brine 4 pieces at a time, letting some of the brine drip off. Dredge the rabbit in the dry mix, and one by one, place the pieces in the oil. Fry the rabbit for 3 minutes, then gently flip the pieces and fry for another 2 to 3 minutes, until it is golden. Remove the rabbit with a slotted spoon or spider, place it on the wire rack, and immediately season with salt.

Repeat the breading and frying process with the remaining rabbit. When all the rabbit has been fried, season again with salt. Place on a serving platter and serve with pickles and mayonnaise.

Chris began his career where he grew up, on Martha's Vineyard, so I was already thinking about islands. I picked a song that combined two of them: "Can It Be All So Simple (Remix)" by Raekwon, which takes one of Wu-Tang's biggest and best hits and outfits it with new lyrics. Neither of the two islands is Martha's Vineyard. One is Staten Island, which gave us the Wu-Tang Clan, and the other is Cuba, which gave us the title of the album, *Only Built 4 Cuban Linx*. There's an added bonus, which is that Raekwon's nickname is The Chef, and a second added bonus, which is that the song is a remix, an example of how basic ingredients can be reused to create something that's newly inspiring.

HOW to FRY A Rabbit

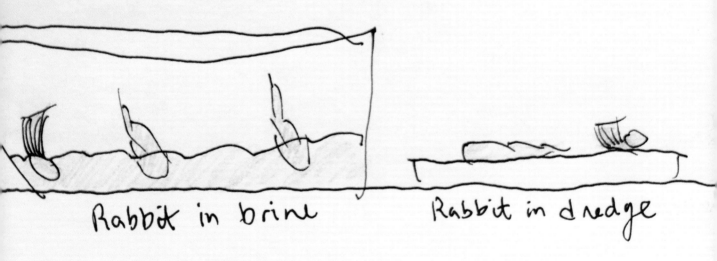

Rabbit in brine   Rabbit in dredge

Rabbit Ready to Fry

Rabbit Frying

FRIED Rabbit

Fried Rabbit drawing by Chris Fischer (recipe previous page)

BITTERSWEET

ENDING

Back in the late nineties, the Roots started to
work with a chef named Terry, who had cooked
at a jazz club in Philly. Terry was a big proponent
of serving drinks early in an event. If they were
delicious and plentiful, then you could please
your guests even before they started to eat. He
got that lesson from going to Chinese buffets
after church; the drinks are endless before you
eat, before they release you to the food. I have
modified Terry's advice: I want people to eat,
but not so much that they ruin dessert.

Blueberry Crunch Cake

Jessica Biel

Serves: 12 to 16
Prep time: 10 minutes
Cook time: 1 hour

This is a kind of dump cake, which is far more appetizing than it sounds: all it means is that you dump the ingredients in a pan and go. And it is a straight-up crowd-pleaser. Asking "Who doesn't like blueberry crunch cake?" is like asking "Who doesn't like apple pie?" or "Who doesn't like ice cream?" or "Who doesn't like crowd-pleasers?" No one. No one. No one.

– ½ cup (1 stick/113 g) unsalted
  butter or margarine,
  plus more for the pan
– 1 (20-ounce/567-g) can crushed
  pineapple
– 3 cups (444 g) fresh blueberries
– 1 box yellow cake mix
– 1½ cups (180 g) chopped pecans
– 2 tablespoons sugar

Preheat the oven to 350°F (175°C) and butter a 9 by 13-inch (23 by 33-cm) baking dish.

Turn the can of pineapple out into the prepared baking dish and top with the blueberries.

Open up the bag of cake mix and add ½ cup (53 g) of the chopped pecans to the bag. Give the bag a few shakes to evenly distribute the pecans. Sprinkle the cake mix evenly over the blueberries.

Melt the butter in a small saucepan, then drizzle the melted butter on top of the cake mix.

Add the remaining 1 cup (110 g) chopped pecans to the pan that the butter was melted in. Toss the buttery pecans with the sugar, then sprinkle them evenly over the cake.

Bake the cake for 1 hour, rotating once halfway through. The cake will be light golden brown on top.

Jessica was born in Ely, Minnesota, in the frozen north, but she moved around frequently in her childhood. The people I know who had similar childhoods have told me that it's important to find certain things that create a sense of rootedness or familiarity, and that food is one of the most powerful examples of this principle. It can take a house and turn it into a home. Jessica is an active cook in her own home now. In light of that, I sent her "A House Is Not a Home," Burt Bacharach and Hal David's iconic explanation of the difference. There are hundreds of versions, many excellent, but I chose the towering one by Luther Vandross. It's rich and satisfying and has so many crescendos that it seems like the end of something: dessert.

Serves: 10 to 12
Prep time: 15 minutes
Cook time: None!

Fruit Salad with Cucumber and Mint
Melody Ehsani

Melody Ehsani was originally slated to go to law school, like lots of the other people in her Persian American family, but she wouldn't do it. She left and began to pursue her own vision, which included lots of designs: streetwear, footwear, and especially jewelry. She's amazing with color—how it's used, how it affects the person who's using it—and my mind immediately went to the hip-hop group Run the Jewels, which has been innovative in its use of color on its album covers. I sent her a track off the Run the Jewels cat-themed remix, *Meow the Jewels*: "Pawfluffer Night," a feline retake of "Blockbuster Night." I also like it because it's a joke, and I'll do anything to get Melody to laugh: her laugh is one of my favorite sounds of all time.

When it comes to fruit, sometimes the best thing to do is to pick your ingredients carefully and then focus on presentation. Nature does the rest. That's certainly the case for Melody's fruit salad. This is true color theory and proof of that theory all in one.

- 16 ounces (about 2½ cups/454 g) strawberries, hulled and quartered
- 3 apples, your favorite variety, cored and chopped
- 1 pound (454 g) Persian cucumbers, chopped
- 6 ounces (170 g) fresh blueberries
- 6 ounces (170 g) fresh blackberries, halved
- 1 Meyer lemon
- 1 bunch mint, leaves picked and torn
- 2 teaspoons flaky salt

Combine the strawberries, apples, cucumbers, blueberries, and blackberries in a large salad bowl.

Using a Microplane, zest the lemon over the salad. Cut the lemon in half and squeeze the juice over the salad.

Add the torn mint leaves and 1 teaspoon of the salt and toss gently to combine. Sprinkle with remaining 1 teaspoon salt and serve.

Cinnamon Rolls with Honey Mead Icing
Dominique Ansel

Serves: 15 to 20
Prep time: 1 hour, plus 4½ hours rising and resting
Cook time: 30 minutes

Sometimes you know how delicious a dessert is going to be just from looking at it. And sometimes a meal needs to end with a sweet, sticky thing.

For the Dough:
- 1⅓ cups (167 g) all-purpose flour, plus more for the work surface
- 1 teaspoon salt
- 2 tablespoons granulated sugar
- 1 teaspoon active dry yeast
- 2 teaspoons milk
- 3 large eggs
- ½ cup (1 stick/113 g) unsalted butter, cubed and softened
- Nonstick cooking spray

For the Cinnamon Schmear:
- 6 tablespoons (¾ stick/85 g) unsalted butter, cubed and softened
- ⅔ cup (138 g) light brown sugar
- 3½ teaspoons ground cinnamon
- 1 large egg white

For the Soak:
- 1 cup (240 ml) whole milk
- 1½ tablespoons unsalted butter, melted and cooled
- 1¼ cups (313 ml) heavy cream
- 5 large eggs, beaten
- ⅓ cup (80 ml) maple syrup
- ¼ teaspoon salt
- ¼ teaspoon lemon zest

For the Icing:
- 1½ cups (165 g) powdered sugar
- 3 tablespoons mead

The Ohio Players' "Sweet Sticky Thing" is a song about different kinds of sugar: sweet taste and also sweet love. I was about five years old when I first heard the song, and I didn't think of it as anything salacious, even though the cover photo showed a naked woman. I was innocent about it, and about what it represented, or at the very least I might have thought that all kinds of plea-sure—the pleasure of a good song sung well, and of sweet food, and anything else—were sort of the same. I want to throw this out as inspiration and see what happens when sweetness in a song meets a chef who is known for bringing the world more sweetness.

To make the dough: Combine the flour, salt, granulated sugar, and yeast in the bowl of a stand mixer fitted with the dough hook attachment. Mix on low speed to combine.

Add the milk, then add 1 egg and continue to mix on low. Increase the speed to medium, add the remaining 2 eggs, then increase the speed to medium-high and mix for 8 to 9 minutes, until the dough begins to pull from the sides of the bowl.

Add the butter a few cubes at a time, incorporating each addition before adding more. Mix until the dough begins to look shiny.

Lightly coat a medium bowl with cooking spray. Remove the dough from the mixer and form it into a ball. Transfer the dough to a bowl and cover with plastic wrap. Press the plastic wrap onto the ball directly to prevent a skin from forming.

(recipe continues on following page)

Let the dough rise for 1 to 1½ hours in a warm place until doubled in size. Cover the dough once again and place in the fridge to chill the dough for at least 3 hours or up to overnight.

To make the schmear: In a medium bowl, whisk all the ingredients until fully incorporated. Cover tightly and set aside until ready to use.

To make the soak: In a large bowl, whisk all the ingredients until fully incorporated.

To form and bake the rolls: Preheat the oven to 350°F (175°C) and line a baking sheet with parchment. Lightly coat a 9-inch (23-cm) round baking dish with cooking spray.

Dust your work surface and rolling pin with flour. Roll the dough out into a ¼-inch (6-mm)-thick rectangle.

Spread a generous amount of the cinnamon schmear evenly across the dough with a spatula, leaving a 1-inch (2.5-cm) border at the top edge.

Roll the dough from the bottom up into a long horizontal log and cut it into ½-inch (12-mm) slices. Place the rolls cut-side up onto the prepared baking sheet at least 1 inch (2.5 cm) apart.

Bake until light golden brown, 15 to 20 minutes. Remove them from the oven and let cool for 10 minutes.

Quickly dunk the rolls in the cinnamon roll soak. Arrange the rolls snugly in the baking dish so the sides are touching one another. Return the dish to the oven and bake for 8 to 10 minutes more, until golden brown

Remove from the oven and let cool for 10 to 15 minutes.

Make the honey mead icing and frost the rolls: In a small bowl, whisk the powdered sugar and mead to dissolve the sugar. Transfer the icing to a zip-top bag or piping bag and cut a small hole at the tip.

Drizzle the rolls with the icing and serve.

Corny Shortcakes with Strawberries and Sour Whipped Cream
Christina Tosi

Serves: 8
Prep time: 30 minutes, plus up to overnight resting
Cook time: 10 minutes

Some desserts are no assembly required. Christina's requires a little bit: the shortcake, the strawberries, the cream. The process of putting it together slightly delays the moment of eating it, which increases the anticipation and the belief that it will be delicious. It is.

Christina is synonymous with milk (she founded and owns Milk Bar, the bakery arm of Momofuku). I had to send her "Milk N' Honey," from the great soul singer Teena Marie. The song features both Gail Gotti and Teena's daughter Rose LaBeau. There's a huge amount of female power in the song—ingenuity, pleasure, and control. It should also be a little sad, because the album it was on, *Congo Square*, would be Teena's last album before she passed in 2010, but the song is too sweetly joyful for that.

For the Shortcakes:
– 1 large egg
– ½ cup (120 ml) heavy cream
– ¾ cup (94 g) all-purpose flour
– ½ cup (57 g) corn flour
– ¼ cup (60 g) freeze-dried corn powder
– ½ cup (100 g) granulated sugar
– ⅓ cup (73 g) light brown sugar
– 1 tablespoon salt
– 1½ teaspoons baking powder
– ½ cup (1 stick/113 g) unsalted butter, cubed
– ¼ cup (56 g) vegetable shortening, at room temperature
– ½ cup (77 g) fresh corn kernels (optional; when in season)
– ½ cup (63 g) confectioners' sugar

For the Strawberries:
– 4 cups (665 g) fresh strawberries, hulled and quartered
– ¼ cup (50 g) granulated sugar

For the Sour Whipped Cream:
– 1½ cups (375 g) heavy cream
– ½ cup (96 g) sour cream
– ½ cup (63 g) confectioners' sugar
– Pinch of salt

To make the shortcakes: Crack the egg into a small liquid measuring cup and whisk it well. You will only need half an egg for this recipe, so remove half of the whisked egg from the measuring cup and reserve it for another use. Add the cream to the remaining egg in the measuring cup until you have ½ cup (120 ml). Whisk to combine and refrigerate while you continue with the recipe.

In the bowl of a stand mixer fitted with the paddle attachment, combine the all-purpose flour, corn flour, freeze-dried corn powder, granulated sugar, brown sugar, salt, and baking powder. Mix on the lowest speed to combine the dry ingredients, then add the butter, shortening, and corn kernels, if using. Mix until you have pea-size lumps, about 4 minutes.

(recipe continues on following page)

Remove the egg mixture from the refrigerator and stream it into the batter until just barely combined. Let the batter rest for 10 minutes. Scoop the batter into 8 balls about 2 tablespoons each and place them on a baking sheet. Chill for at least 30 minutes or up to overnight.

Meanwhile, make the strawberries: Put the hulled strawberries and sugar in a medium bowl and toss to combine. Let the strawberries sit for an hour or two before serving, tossing occasionally.

To bake the shortcakes: Preheat the oven to 350°F (175°C) and line a baking sheet with parchment. Place the confectioners' sugar in a shallow bowl and roll each shortcake through the sugar to evenly coat. Tap off the excess and place the shortcakes on the prepared baking sheet, leaving enough space between each so they can double in size.

Bake for 9 to 11 minutes, until the sugar begins to look cracked and the shortcakes have spread quite a bit. Leave on the sheet until cool enough to handle, then transfer the shortcakes to a cooling rack.

To make the sour whipped cream: Combine the heavy cream, sour cream, confectioners' sugar, and salt in the bowl of a stand mixer and whisk on medium speed until soft peaks form. Don't overwhip!

To serve: Place the shortcakes on a serving platter and top each with about ½ cup (83 g) of the strawberries. Pour the remaining juices over everything, top with the whipped cream, and serve immediately.

Christina's tip: Freeze-dried corn powder can be ordered from the internet.

Tiramisu Tradizionale

Joey Baldino

Serves: 12 to 16
Prep time: 30 minutes,
plus at least 1 hour refrigerating
Cook time: None!

Joey's tiramisu comes out of a pan, after which cocoa powder gets sprinkled on top. It's like "pan" au chocolat. (I know it's *pain*. This is a joke that only works if you say it out loud.) And you can put it in the freezer for up to a week.

- 8 large eggs, yolks and whites separated
- 1½ cups (300 g) sugar
- 16 ounces (454 g) mascarpone cheese
- 4 cups (1 L) strong coffee or espresso, cooled
- 2 (17.5-ounce/496 g) packages Italian ladyfingers (about 120); reserve half for serving
- 3 tablespoons cocoa powder

In an electric mixer using the whisk attachment, whip the egg yolks with 1 cup (200 g) of the sugar until thick and pale in color.

In a separate, clean mixing bowl fitted with the paddle attachment, whip the mascarpone cheese just until soft. Add the egg yolk mixture and mix until combined.

Thoroughly clean out the first mixing bowl and dry it. Add the egg whites and the remaining ½ cup (100 g) sugar and whip with the whisk attachment until the mixture can hold a peak at the end of a whisk.

Using a rubber spatula, fold the whipped whites into the mascarpone mixture in three additions. Fill a piping bag with the mascarpone mousse.

Place the cooled coffee in a shallow bowl and very quickly dip a few ladyfingers at a time in and out of the coffee, then place them side by side in a 9 by 13-inch (23 by 33-cm) baking dish. Once you have completed a full layer, evenly pipe one third of the mascarpone mousse in a single layer on top of the ladyfingers. Repeat twice to make three layers of dipped ladyfingers and mascarpone mousse. Dust 2 tablespoons cocoa powder through a fine-mesh sieve over the top of the dish. Refrigerate for at least 1 hour or up to overnight before serving.

To serve, scoop into a sundae glass followed by a ladyfinger and a dusting of cocoa.

South Philly, where Joey Baldino cooks, is a historically Italian American enclave. It's where Frankie Avalon hails from, and Jim Croce, and Rocky Balboa (at least in some of the movies). But when I was coming up, South Philly meant hip-hop. We busked there. Beanie Sigel came from there too. Many of Beanie's songs are battle tracks, and I'm sending Joey one of the most obvious: "Where's My Opponent." Chefs often cook the same dishes as other chefs, and while they don't want others to fail, they want to do something to their dish that elevates it above the rest. Competitiveness, at least for motivational purposes, is part of the deal, like it is in any art form.

RAISE A

GLASS

The human body is seventy percent water, as is the planet. Your dinner party shouldn't be quite that, but drinks are still important. Guests need to stay hydrated, or to have something in their hand if they're circulating at a point in the evening when they're away from food (either because they haven't moved on to the next course, or because they're taking a self-imposed break). These drinks, both alcoholic and not, will help you keep things fluid.

Ginger Beer
Thelma Golden

Serves: 10 to 12
Prep time: 15 minutes,
plus 2 to 3 days fermenting
Cook time: None!

Thelma's mother used to make this ginger beer, and Thelma has agreed to pass the recipe along to those of us who aren't in the family. This is one of those drinks that's not hard to make but does require some prep time and foresight. I, for one, am a huge fan of ginger beer, so I would like to thank both Thelma and her mother.

- 2 (3-inch/7.6-cm) pieces fresh ginger,
  peeled and roughly chopped
- 2 quarts (1.8 L), plus 1 cup (240 ml) water
- 1 cup (200 g) sugar
- Lime wedges
- 3 limes

Place ginger in a large saucepan and add 2 quarts (1.8 L) water. Bring to a boil over high heat and then lower the heat to simmer until it is potent, at least 15 minutes or up to 2 hours. Remove from the heat, cool completely, then pour into a clean jar or ceramic or other nonreactive container.

In a small pot, combine the sugar with 1 cup (240 ml) water and bring to a boil to make a simple syrup. Remove from the heat and let cool, then add it to the vessel with the ginger brew.

Place a lid over the vessel and allow to ferment at room temperature for 2 to 3 days, opening it once a day to release some of the gases, until it is bubbling and active.

Strain the ginger beer through a fine-mesh sieve into a pitcher. Serve during cocktail hour in champagne flutes with a lime garnish.

Thelma is the Director and Chief Curator of the Studio Museum in Harlem. For decades she has shown the city's and the country's top African American artists while keeping track of great artists from the past. Something about Thelma's approach reminds me of Solange's "Fuck the Industry," which is not a profane song at all, but rather a principled statement of creative identity. Solange explains that she's not Beyoncé, that she's not Ashanti, that she's not anyone else. What's left is her and her alone. And you can't go wrong with a Solange song, Hadley Street or otherwise.

Bourbon Raspberry Tea
Gabrielle Union

Whenever I'm in Miami, I see Gabrielle. I also hear Miami bass, and that leads me to "Whoot, There It Is!" by 95 South, which came out in April of 1993 and got into the Billboard Top 20. A month later, another Miami bass group, Tag Team, came out with "Whoomp! (There It Is)," which got all the way up to number two. If you've heard one version, it's likely the Tag Team one, but the songs remain a fascinating example of inspiration, copying, and close-cousin creativity—all of which are players in cooking as well. (There's also a small domestic drama tucked into the musical choice: 95 South contributed to the soundtrack of Gabrielle's cheerleader comedy *Bring It On*, and her husband, Dwyane Wade's, team, the Miami Heat, has used the Tag Team song to rev up the crowd.)

This is a very refreshing drink, not too sweet, with just the right amount of kick. Feel free to adjust the level of alcohol depending on the length and tone of your party. I tend to aim for the lower end of the spectrum, but you may have a different approach.

– 2 cups (432 g) 4C Raspberry Iced Tea
  Mix, or preferred brand
– 1½ gallons (5.7 L) water
– 1 (750-ml) bottle bourbon,
  or rye whisky if preferred
– Fresh raspberries, for garnish

Combine the iced tea mix and the water in a large punch bowl or pitcher. Stir well to dissolve the mix. Add the bourbon and stir well to combine. Serve over ice with fresh raspberries for garnish.

Serves: 10 to 20
Prep time: 5 minutes,
plus 7 to 10 days infusing
Cook time: None!

Kether's Favorite Cocktail: "Me and Mia"
(from Tramp Stamp Granny's Bar in LA)
Kether Donohue

Kether acts and Kether sings, and she does both equally well. Some roles call for both at the same time: she's been in *Pitch Perfect* and *Grease Live*. I decided to pick a song for her that communicated the same sense of exuberance and energy that she does, and that was why I ended up at Little Richard's "Rip It Up," one of the best examples of an unstoppable voice that starts at a thousand miles an hour and never slows down.

You know when the taste of truffle is just too overpowering to eat, let alone drink? Have no fear, friends: this is a well-balanced and highbrow cocktail that is perfect at the end of a long meal.

- 2 cups (480 ml) bourbon
- 2 tablespoons white truffle flakes
- 1 (750-ml) bottle Carpano Antica vermouth
- 1 (750-ml) bottle Amontillado sherry
- Truffle salt
- 6 lemons, each cut into 8 wedges
- Ice cubes

Pour the bourbon into a glass pint jar. Add the truffle flakes, cover tightly, and let infuse in a cool place away from sunlight for 7 to 10 days. Strain.

Pour the vermouth, sherry, and infused bourbon into a large punch bowl. Place a dish of truffle salt next to the punch bowl along with the lemon wedges.

Instruct guest to swipe the rim of their glass with the lemon wedge, then dip the rim into the truffle salt. Fill the glass to the brim with ice and ladle the cocktail over the ice. It's a strong one, so the ice is key!

Serves: 1
Prep time: 15 minutes
Cook time: 25 minutes
(for the Homemade Syrup)

Red Skies at Night
Dave Arnold

Dave Arnold has done great things at the intersection of food and science. He once cooked a turkey inside out, and another time he created cocktails in a centrifuge. I sent him "Sounds of Science" by the Beastie Boys, which is hyperkinetic and verbally dense. It suggests a million ideas and makes all of them happen at once. As the song says, "expanding the horizons and expanding the parameters."

Science may have been the impetus behind Dave's drink, but art was the result. You are all seeing this cocktail in a pristine photograph that makes it look like something from a jewelry ad, but it looked like that in real life too. There's something about the concentration at the bottom versus the concentration at the top that makes it look like a sand painting, or a sunrise, or a Georgia O'Keeffe.

– Cocktail ice
– 1 tablespoon fresh lime juice
– 1¾ ounces (50 ml) Flor de Caña or other white rum
– Soda water
– 1 lime slice

For the Homemade Syrup:
Makes enough for 40 drinks
– 2 (2-inch/5-cm) pieces turmeric root, roughly chopped
– 2 (2-inch/5-cm) pieces fresh ginger, rougly chopped
– 3¼ cups (130 g) wildflower honey
– 3¼ cups (780 ml) water
– 2 teaspoons red chile flakes
– 2 ounces (57 g) vegetable glycerin
– ½ teaspoon salt

To make the syrup: Bring all of the syrup ingredients to a boil, then reduce to a simmer for 5 minutes. Let cool completely and then transfer to a heat proof vessel for pouring.

To make each drink: Fill a glass with ice. Add the syrup, lime juice, and rum and stir at least 10 times to dissolve the syrup. Top with soda, stir again, and finish with a slice of lime.

TER PARTY: SNACKS

One of the things about a potluck is that you can never be sure when it will end. People lounge. People linger. People swear they are full and then get hungry again. For all those reasons, late-night snacks are the secret weapon of a good potluck, and they let you both serve up comfort food and experiment. That's the role of snacks. They're sites of creative risk that reward the people who have stuck around until the end. They're finger foods that light up the mind. There's a Wonka dimension to them.

Grilled Bologna Sliders on Hawaiian Rolls
Matty Matheson

Serves: 12
Prep time: 5 minutes
Cook time: 20 minutes

Matty is a slider expert, and this dish is a perfect illustration of his expertise. Sliders are bite-size, so they're able to do things with taste that full-size hamburgers cannot.

- 12 pack of King's Hawaiian Sweet Rolls
- ½ cup (215 g) mayonnaise
- 1 tablespoon mustard of choice
- ½ dill pickle, diced
- ¼ white onion, diced
- Salt
- 12 (¼-inch-/6-mm-thick) slices bologna (ask your deli counter to slice it)
- 2 tablespoons neutral oil, such as canola or vegetable
- 12 slices American cheese
- Shredded iceberg lettuce (optional)

Preheat a large cast-iron skillet over medium heat. Separate the rolls.

Make the sauce by mixing together the mayonnaise, mustard, dill pickle, and onion. Season with salt.

Use a biscuit cutter or glass just bigger than the diameter of the rolls to cut the bologna into slider-size pieces.

Fill a large pot with 2 inches (5 cm) of water and place a steamer basket inside. Cover and bring the water to a simmer over medium heat.

Place the rolls in the hot steamer basket and steam for 3 minutes, or until hot.

Meanwhile, heat 1 tablespoon of the oil in the preheated skillet. Add half of the bologna slices and pan-fry until the edges are golden brown, about 2 to 3 minutes. Place a slice of cheese over each slice of bologna and cook until just melted. Repeat with the remaining oil, bologna, and cheese.

Spread a nice amount of sauce on each bun. Sandwich the bologna and melted cheese into the rolls, add the lettuce, if using, and serve.

I was fortunate enough to have Matty participate in one of my Food Salons in New York. I was consistently impressed by the way he wove together serious topics and those that were not so serious. He talked about his family and how food was a unifying force early in his life. He talked about moving from a small town to Toronto and taking in the energy of the city. He talked about the stresses of a chef's life. We also talked about sneakers, which we both collect, and which raise some of the same creative issues as food—how to innovate while also respecting tradition, for example. This was still in my mind when I asked him to join in on the potluck, which is why I'm sending him Run-D.M.C.'s "My Adidas," one of the legendary songs about shoes, stress, energy, and unifying forces.

Eggs in Purgatory
Stanley Tucci

Serves: 8 to 10
Prep time: 5 minutes
Cook time: 40 minutes

In life, and in books, I am somewhat loath to go for the obvious. But sometimes it's irresistible. And this is one of those cases. Stanley has done lots about food in his career and is an expert at explaining the role of food in Italian culture. This springs from one source: the 1996 movie *Big Night*. Tucci played the co-owner of Paradise, a restaurant on the Jersey Shore in the 1950s. Secondo, Tucci's character, is at odds with his brother Primo (Tony Shalhoub) over the future of Paradise. The movie is filled with food and music, and in one of the most famous scenes, Paradise's staff dances to "Mambo Italiano," sung by Rosemary Clooney.

Stanley's dish should be made on-site. Bring the prepared sauce over in a jar along with a carton of eggs, and if you sense that your late-night crowd needs more sustenance, fire it up. It can also serve as a lighter snack to satiate any late-night cravings so you won't feel bad the next day even if you're eating into the wee hours.

- ¼ cup (60 ml) extra-virgin olive oil, plus more to finish
- 1 large yellow onion, chopped
- 2 cloves garlic, thinly sliced
- 3 pepperoncini, chopped (optional)
- 1 (28-ounce/709-g) can whole peeled San Marzano tomatoes
- 2 teaspoons salt, plus more to taste
- Leaves from 1 small bunch basil
- Freshly ground black pepper
- Warmed fresh Italian bread, for serving

Heat the oil in an extra-large sauté pan or cast-iron skillet over medium heat until shimmering. Add the onion and garlic and cook until softened but not colored, about 8 minutes. If using the pepperoncini, add it now.

Empty the can of tomatoes into a medium bowl and crush well using your hands. Add the tomatoes to the pan, then add 1 teaspoon of the salt and half of the basil leaves.

Bring to a boil and stir well, then decrease the heat to low, cover, and simmer for 30 minutes.

Uncover and make 8 divots as evenly apart as possible with a bit of space in between and place your eggs in the divots. Cover and cook just until the whites are set and the yolks are still runny, 7 to 10 minutes.

Sprinkle with the remaining 1 teaspoon salt and season with pepper. Drizzle with a few glugs of oil and top with the remaining basil.

Serve hot with thick slices of warm Italian bread.

Tucci's tip: Feel free to serve this with a little cheese—Parm works great.

Mac and Cheese
Q-Tip

Serves: 6 to 8
Prep time: 20 minutes
Cook time: 30 minutes

You can make this up to two days ahead of time and then heat it for the party. That makes it a peace-of-mind dish. And you can substitute different cheeses, though I wouldn't tamper too much with this recipe, as Tip has calibrated it to perfection. Seriously: I've never had better mac and cheese.

- 2 tablespoons unsalted butter, softened, for the pan
- 2 cups (194 g) grated Asiago cheese
- 1½ cups (170 g) grated white Cheddar cheese
- 1½ cups (146 g) grated American Cheddar
- 1 cup (97 g) grated Fontina cheese
- ½ cup (50 g) grated Parmesan cheese
- 1 tablespoon olive oil
- 4 jalapeño peppers, thinly sliced into rings
- 4 cloves garlic, finely chopped
- 5 cups (1.2 L) whole milk
- 3 tablespoons all-purpose flour
- 4 large egg yolks, whisked
- 2 teaspoons fresh thyme leaves, finely chopped
- ½ teaspoon cayenne pepper
- Salt
- ½ teaspoon freshly ground black pepper
- 1 pound (454) fresh sausage—Italian, chorizo, or dealer's choice
- 1 pound (454 g) elbow macaroni

I have tried to respect a rule of not sending people songs on which they themselves appeared. It's been hard, though. And now I'm going to start breaking it. Why? Because when a person agrees to contribute to a cookbook, and that person is a founding member of a legendary hip-hop group, A Tribe Called Quest, that has recorded—along with its songs about community, spirituality, and political reality—songs about food, the tendency is to choose one of them. I did. I can't think of Q-Tip and food without thinking of "Ham 'N' Eggs." The song was one of the first conscious rap anthems I ever heard, mostly because it did what no one else had dared to do: it took those childhood foods that all of us held dear and held them up to nutritional scrutiny.

(recipe continues on following page)

Preheat the oven to 375°F (190°C). Butter the bottom and sides of a baking dish (preferably 10 by 10 inches [25 by 25 cm] but 9 by 13 inches [23 by 33 cm] will work as well).

Combine ¼ cup (24 g) of each cheese in a small bowl and set aside for later.

Heat the oil in a Dutch oven or other heavy-bottomed large saucepan over medium heat. Add the jalapeños and cook for about 1 minute, until lightly colored. Add the garlic and stir until fragrant, about 30 seconds.

Meanwhile, pour the milk into a small saucepan and warm over medium heat; be careful not to let it boil.

Whisk the flour into the jalapeño-garlic mixture, then very slowly whisk in the hot milk. Cook, whisking constantly, for about 5 minutes, until combined and no lumps remain in the flour. Slowly add the whisked egg yolks and cook for an additional 1 to 2 minutes, or until completely combined and slightly thickened.

Remove the sauce from the heat and whisk in the thyme, cayenne, and all of the remaining cheeses until they are completely incorporated. Add ½ teaspoon salt and the black pepper; taste and adjust the seasoning if needed.

If using sausage, remove it from the casing and cook in a medium sauté pan over medium heat until fully cooked and browned.

Bring a medium pot of water to a boil, salt the water, then add the macaroni and cook for 7 minutes, or until al dente.

Drain the macaroni and fold it into the sauce, then turn it out into the prepared baking dish. Stir in the sausage, if using. Top with the reserved cheese.

Place in the oven and bake for 10 to 15 minutes, then serve.

Tina's Cold "Pizza"
Jarobi White

Jarobi was in A Tribe Called Quest for the first record, *People's Instinctive Travels and the Paths of Rhythm*, and then left for a while to pursue—of all things—cooking. I'm going to take a slight left turn here and send him "Pease Porridge," which isn't a Tribe song but comes from elsewhere in the Native Tongues Posse, from De La Soul. It's about food, to some degree, but also about peace and consciousness and community. So here I go, breaking the rule a second time. It won't happen again.

This dish is easy to transport. It's also ideal for the end of the party. Right when everyone starts to grumble that all the good snacks are gone, pull out this pizza. Doesn't need heating. Doesn't need time. Needs only hungry mouths to feed. Seriously, dudes—you can't skimp on this dish; it's the fancy pizza you needed to meet.

– 1 (8-ounce/227-g) package cream cheese, softened
– ¾ cup (180 ml) Heinz Chili sauce
– ½ onion, diced
– 1 green bell pepper, diced
– ½ cup (67 g) sliced black olives
– 1 pound (454 g) frozen and thawed cooked shrimp, chopped
– 1 cup (118 g) cooked lump crabmeat
– 1½ cups (165 g) grated mozzarella cheese
– 1 (1-ounce/28-g) packet taco seasoning

Spread the cream cheese evenly and to the edges of a round serving dish or large plate to act as the crust. Spread the chili sauce on top of the cream cheese, like the sauce on a pizza. Be gentle here; you don't want the layers to mix.

Top with the onion, pepper, olives, shrimp, and lump crabmeat. Follow with the cheese.

Chill everything for at least 30 minutes and up to 3 hours.

Remove the "pizza" from the fridge and finish with the taco seasoning. Serve with your favorite cracker or chip—something that has some structure to stand up to the dip, such as a pita chip or Triscuit.

Serves: 6 to 8
Prep time: 10 minutes
Cook time: 20 minutes

"Heimy's Happiness" Fries with Kewpie Mayo, Caviar, (and a Glass of Bubbles)
Eric Wareheim

I wasn't sure what aspect of Eric's career I should focus on when I sent him his musical prompt. His stand-up comedy? His music? His acting? I decided to look at Eric the director, and in particular, Eric the director of music videos. He's done some of the strangest and most visionary videos of recent years, and there's no better example of this than Major Lazer's "Bubble Butt." It has to be seen to be believed, but just know that it has inflatable rears, women who explode into confetti, and a flying giantess. I can't send Eric that song—it doesn't directly violate the rule I have already violated twice, but it's close—so I sent a close cousin, James Brown's "For Goodness Sakes, Look at Those Cakes." It could be about regular old cakes, right? Stage whisper: It isn't.

Eric is known for his maximalist way with food and drink. In addition to having a dozen-plus jobs—actor, comedian, director, writer, and musician (I can sympathize)—Eric makes natural wines in Sonoma, California. His favorite thing to bring to a potluck is a bottle of his Las Jaras Sparkling. Make it Heimy time with this decadent addition.

– 1 bag frozen french fries
– Kewpie mayonnaise
– 1 (3.5-ounce/100-g) jar caviar
– Sparkling wine, preferably Las Jaras

Cook the french fries according to the package instructions. Remove from the oven and place them in coupes. Squeeze your desired amount of mayo over the top, followed by a "neat" dollop or two of caviar.

Serve alongside a glass of sparkling wine.

Heimy's tip: Kewpie mayonese is a Japanese mayo that is made with rice vinegar, which gives it a distinct flavor. It's loved by foodies—leave the bottle as a host gift.

AFTERWORD

Potluck Guest
Janina Gavankar

If You Can't Cook, You Still Can Help.

I wanted a sense of community in this mixtape meal. As the song I gave myself in the introduction says, everybody eats when they come to my house. But as Martha Stewart said in her foreword (which, I will admit, I read before I wrote this afterword—is that allowed?), potlucks are about balancing control and loss of control. I found that out early. One of the first people I contacted to contribute to the book was the actress Janina Gavankar. You know her from *Sleepy Hollow*, or from *True Blood*, or from *Pee-Wee's Big Holiday*, where she played a party guest.

Janina was happy to talk to me about the book but a little confused why I was calling her. In fact, she recorded our call. I don't mean that she ran a tape. If I don't know the protocols for who reads what went in a book, I certainly don't know the protocols for one-party and two-party taping. But she jotted down our conversation, and then sent it back to me as an e-mail. According to her records, it went something like this:

> **Her:** Wait. Why are you calling me for this?
> **Me:** It's a potluck recipe book, J.
> **Her:** So I have to supply a recipe?
> **Me:** Yes. That is how recipe books work.
> **Her:** I can't cook, Ahmir. You know this. Cooking to me is putting popcorn in microwaved tomato soup. Can I copy one from, like, Padma Lakshmi?
> **Me:** She's already doing this book, and that's plagiarism.
> **Her:** [expletive redacted]

After careful consideration, Janina decided to contribute, but on her own terms. She told me that while she was not qualified to cook, she was qualified to be a good guest at a potluck, and that she would prove that by submitting a recipe that was more a promise to bring ice and a plant. She even sent a picture of herself holding both and arriving at a door that I guess is supposed to be my door but is probably her door. She's dressed for the occasion, though, and it's "premium ice," so come on in!

Janina was the only one who customized the assignment, but she reminded me of the importance of putting guests at ease and involving even those guests with a mortal fear of preparing food dishes. So I wanted to offer a few quick tips for a potluck.

Do not have a dress code.
Maybe this seems obvious, but you don't want people to feel like they're living up to a certain standard. Also, people then fall (or rise) to their own comfort level, and that makes for a fascinating jumble. You might get a person in a T-shirt next to a person in a lovely pink-and-gray dress, and that is a narrative all its own.

You can name a starting time, but not an ending time.
As the host, try to think of your potluck as a family event. The guests are not (or are not *only*) family members, but extend them the same courtesy. In other words, expect them to arrive when you say, more or less, but expect some of them to linger. It's why I have included recipes for late-night snacks. By the way, nothing says that you have to be entirely even-tempered about people lingering. You can be irritated in a loving way, as you would for family. I have a story to tell here—a story to tell on myself. In the nineties, I had a house on St. Albans Street in Philadelphia that was the epicenter of various jam sessions. It's where so many people got started: Bilal, Eve, Musiq Soulchild, and so on. People would drop by and play. Sometimes, though, I would come home late at night and find that the jam sessions were still going, with no end in sight. In those cases, I would lock myself in a back room and call in a noise complaint to the police, pretending I was a concerned neighbor. That's right: I would call the cops on my own house. Do not do that unless you are in an emergency situation.

Have games.
This is vital. If people are staying, they're staying to talk, but also to entertain each other. I have game nights at my house, and the games vary over time, from traditional no-apparatus-necessary activities like charades or trivia to high-tech versions like Quiplash to old-fashioned board games like

Monopoly or Othello or Connect Four. Games can be out on the table or on a shallow shelf just under the tabletop, and when they start to come out, be receptive to your party breaking into smaller groups. And encourage your guests to bring or propose their own games. Some of the most enjoyable moments I've had are the result of one of my guests trying to explain their house-rules variation on charades from when they were young. It never goes well, but it always goes very well.

Keep the lighting low but not too low.
Harsh light is good for no one except interrogation subjects. But if the lighting is too low, people can get sleepy or misunderstand and think it's a make-out party. Set your lights on "relaxed fun." Your lights have that as a setting, right?

Have lots of drinks (as I've said), but make sure lots of the drinks you have are nonalcoholic.
It's my preference as a nondrinker, but it's also vital to make sure that your guests, while having a good time, are not led into error. Excessive alcohol can encourage behaviors that put them and other guests at risk of embarrassment or worse. I'm not saying that parties should be dry. I'm just saying that if there's too much alcohol, it can be slippery when wet.

Keep your ears open.
This may seem like a strange tip, but it's vital. As the host, one of your jobs is to connect people in the latticework of the party. If you walk by a conversation about bridge architecture, and three minutes later someone on the other end of the room wonders aloud to you how suspension bridges work, it's incumbent upon you to bring those two conversational strands together. Any good potluck is a tapestry.

Have ice and plants.
Ice keeps things cold, and plants keep things cool. If only I knew someone who could bring me ice and plants. Oh, hi, Janina!

Be mindful of waste.

This piece of advice comes courtesy of the writer and director Mike Birbiglia. I invited Mike to the potluck, and while he didn't send a recipe, he sent a note. I reprint part of it here with his permission. "Don't bring anything that will end up in a landfill. There's too much damn garbage. We should all consider giving people things that they can either eat or keep. For example, you can bring people strawberry shortcake in a really nice Tupperware that they can keep and use again. Or bring over a delicious batch of hot chocolate in a reusable receptacle that they can use again and again. This should be your guideline: if you're not going to take it home with you, make sure that it's nice enough that they would feel bad about throwing it out. The whole thing is mostly about guilt."

Mike's tip is the last tip, not because there's nothing more to say about potlucks, but because it sent me into a reverie. It put me in mind of my grandmom. She didn't host potlucks. She did the cooking herself, but she still managed to make the whole thing feel communal. Partly that's because she was so welcoming, but partly it was because of her ethic, which was about making sure that nothing went to waste. She was big on leftovers, which she kept in emptied-out jars of Hellmann's mayonnaise. She kept the grease and oil from meats, for example. I know she did it just to save on having to buy Wesson oil and Crisco all the time, but it became a part of her cooking. After it hardened overnight, she would use it to make everything. All our Saturday pancakes had beefy overtones. (It wasn't a problem, because we had sausage on the plate, too—it felt like a plan.) The best thing she would make with meat grease was butter cookies, which she cooked extra long. They were the best-tasting cookies ever. Her most famous dish was her potlicker—she took the juice and oil she collected from a month of cabbage, collard greens, and mustard greens and any steamed or boiled vegetable and put them all together.

I went down a rabbit hole there, but now I'm back. My grandmom and her cooking sums up all of these tips about hosting and the events I try to apply them at. She came long before any of these parties, and her way of thinking will be around for a long time after them. She represents a certain time and place and a certain set of habits: frugal living, resourceful creativity, but also cooking with a group in mind, and cooking with the desire to make people feel comfortable, safe, full, and happy. I know that habits have changed. I know the culture has shifted. I know that the things she served back then might be seen as unhealthy today. But it works the way music works. Whenever I hear certain songs, I am transported back to when I first heard them, and all the thoughts and emotions from that first time return to me. My grandmother's cooking has the same effect. So whenever I have people over, whenever I host a potluck, a little part of my mind goes back there. It collects these ideas of community and pleasure and mutual responsibility, brings the past into the present, and helps to make the future.

Oh, one final matter. As I explained in the introduction, I don't cook. I can't cook. But I can cook music. So what I decided to do, in the end, was bring my own recipe in the form of the Ultimate Dinner Party Playlist. Other people brought dishes. I brought a playlist. The next time you have a dinner party, make sure you play this and this alone. Start it exactly one minute before the first guest arrives. For more specific tips and philosophies regarding playlists, keep reading. You'll arrive at them soon enough (page 212, if you're excessively impatient).

MIXTAPE POTLUCK PLAYLIST

Throughout this book, there's been music, most notably in the margins of every recipe. Those songs, of course, were selected for individual contributors. They are the songs I heard in my head when I thought of the guests cooking and then bringing their dishes to the potluck. They were meant as forms of inspiration, as cultural kitchen prep. Enjoy them as you cook, or as you think about cooking.

Éric Ripert
Joshua Redman—*The Ocean*

Camille Becerra
Miles Davis—*Blue in Green*

Carla Hall
Starlito—*Family to Feed*

Nyesha Arrington
Toddy Tee—*Batterram*

Tom Sachs
Billy Preston—*Outa-Space*

Kelly Fields
TBC Brass Band—*Let's Go Get Em*

Fred Armisen
Boogie Down Productions—
The Style You Haven't Done Yet

Maya Rudolph
Muddy Waters—*Herbert Harper's
Free Press News*

Martha Stewart
Snoop Dogg—*Life of Da Party*

Shep Gordon
Son of Bazerk—*Change the Style*

Dustin Yellin
Royce da 5'9"—*Layers*

Tariq Trotter
Lambert, Hendricks & Ross—
Home Cookin'

Ardenia Brown
Goodie Mob—*Soul Food*

Alex Stupak
Akwid—*Es Mi Gusto*

Padma Lakshmi
Jelly Roll Morton and his Red Hot
Peppers—*Red Hot Peppers Stomp*

Lilly Singh
Stevie Wonder—*Superwoman (Where
Were You When I Needed You)*

Greg Baxtrom
Mos Def—*Climb*

Zooey Deschanel
Prince—*Joint 2 Joint*

Ignacio Mattos
Los Shakers—*Break It All*

Marisa Tomei
Audio Two—*Top Billin*

MIXTAPE POTLUCK PLAYLIST

Jessica Seinfeld
Wale—*The Roots Song Wale Is On*

Ashley Graham
Zager & Evans—*In the Year 2525*

Mark Ladner
Lil Wayne—*6 Foot 7 Foot*

Edouardo Jordan
Jill Scott—*Family Reunion*

Humberto Leon
Pizzicato Five—*Past, Present, Future*

Flynn McGarry
Rae Sremmurd (featuring Gucci Mane)—*Black Beatles*

Tanya Holland
Tony! Toni! Toné!—*Let's Get Down*

Jessica Koslow
Method Man and Redman—*Cereal Killer*

Kwame Onwuachi
The Young Senators—*Jungle*

Amy Poehler
Love Unlimited—*It May Be Winter Outside (But in My Heart It's Spring)*

Yvonne Orji
Fela Kuti—*Water No Get Enemy*

Haile Thomas
D'Angelo—*Chicken Grease*

Jimmy Fallon
Bruce Springsteen—*Hungry Heart*

Kimbal Musk
Lenny Kravitz—*I Build This Garden for Us*

Carol Lim
Rufus Thomas—*Do the Funky Penguin*

Natalie Portman
The Beach Boys—*Vegetables*

Kevin Tien
Fats Domino—*Let the Four Winds Blow*

Athena Calderone
LaBelle—*Moon Shadow*

Andrew Zimmern
Rufus (featuring Chaka Khan)—
Egyptian Song

J.J. Johnson
J.J. Johnson—*100 Proof*

Mashama Bailey
Afrika Bambaataa—*Renegades of Funk*

Missy Robbins
Missy Elliott (featuring Lamb)—
I'm Better

Chris Fischer
Raekwon—*Can It Be All So Simple*
(Remix)

Jessica Biel
Luther Vandross—*A House Is
Not a Home*

Melody Ehsani
Run the Jewels—*Pawfluffer Night*

Dominique Ansel
Ohio Players—*Sweet Sticky Thing*

Christina Tosi
Teena Marie (featuring Rose LaBeau,
Gail Gotti)—*Milk N' Honey*

Joey Baldino
Beanie Sigel—*Where's My Opponent*

Thelma Golden
Solange—*Fuck the Industry*

Gabrielle Union
Tag Team—*Whoomp! (There It Is)*

Kether Donohue
Little Richard—*Rip It Up*

Dave Arnold
Beastie Boys—*The Sounds of Science*

Matty Matheson
Run-D.M.C.—*My Adidas*

Stanley Tucci
Rosemary Clooney—*Mambo Italiano*

Q-Tip
A Tribe Called Quest—*Ham 'N' Eggs*

Jarobi White
De La Soul—*Pease Porridge*

Eric Wareheim
James Brown—*For Goodness Sakes,
Look at Those Cakes*

PLAYLIST TIPS

Constructing playlists is something that I encounter on a daily basis. Partly that's because I work as a DJ, a job that I interpret not simply as an opportunity to move the crowd (though that's part of it) but as a chance to create a collage of the world's finest organized noise, a musical history lesson. Songs come together for maximum power, whether it's in a dance club or in an arena before a concert.

Mixtape Potluck

So how do playlists work at a dinner party? They can work very well, but not very simply. Making a playlist, in fact, is both like and unlike hosting a potluck dinner. On the one hand, it involves bringing together other people's creations and arranging them for the enjoyment of a group. On the other hand, potlucks can feel like excruciating exercises in loss of control, at least from the food side: if you're the host, you can hint at what people should bring, but you can never fully orchestrate the meal. Playlists allow full control, in a sense—though you aren't making the songs so much as collecting them, you don't have to worry about surprising ingredients, or instructions for preparation, or even an unexpected taste. That song by The Time—or A Tribe Called Quest, or Missy Elliott, or Curtis Mayfield, or Teena Marie—sounds the same every time. The job is one of curation. What should come first? What should follow it? How are you setting the mood, managing it, driving the dinner party from its inception to its conclusion? What emotions and ideas are you releasing into the room?

Here are some tips for creating the best dinner party playlist:

Build slow.
Whatever time you think your party is starting, that's not exactly when it's starting. Make sure you program some arrival music that doesn't demand an excessive amount of attention. Jazz works well, or instrumental hip-hop. Everyone will be making introductions. Don't confuse this time of casual small talk by adding lyrics to the mix.

Balance self-portraiture with the instinct to entertain.
When I try to reach an audience, whether in a club or a dining room, I want them to have a good time, but I want them to have a good time on my terms. I don't mean that arrogantly. It's not all about me. But if I'm throwing a dinner party, if I'm calling it for a certain time, if I'm making the guest list and picking the decor, I'm also damn sure going to control the music. Don't be ashamed to think of the party as a canvas, and the playlist as both brush and paints.

Pick music that reinforces the narrative of the evening.
This is a variation of the earlier tip, but it's an important tip, so nice I'm saying it twice. A dinner party, like everything else that people do, is a psychological experience. In a potluck, you will not be controlling the food, but you can control other things. You can work the room's lighting to the advantage of the evening—the same goes for temperature and the organization of the furniture. And, of course, the music. You can bring people from an early state of excited anticipation through a state of satisfaction to a state of pleased departure if you pick your music correctly. I can't be too specific here—not just because they're trade secrets, but because every party is slightly different—but there are some general guidelines. Vary tempos. Alternate between new music and nostalgic favorites. Music is not only entertainment, but a way of keeping time and regulating biorhythms. For example, think of a party that leans into sixties soul: that kind of music feels communal, and even when you turn it down, you can hear the pulse, whether it's James Jamerson with the Funk Brothers or someone else. It keeps time and keeps people present in time. You don't need synesthesia to see that different music gives off different-colored glows.

Throw some curveballs as the night progresses.
In my DJ sets, I have moments that I use as Rorschach tests—I like to throw out unexpected songs and see how they land. It might be the *Golden Girls* theme, or an edit of Phil Collins's "In the Air Tonight" that cuts off right before the drum solo. In those moments, you can see the crowd redivide itself into those who get the joke and those who do not, those who feel spoken to and those who feel excluded from the moment. Midway through your dinner party, do something like that. Maybe follow Bobby Caldwell's "What You Won't Do for Love" with Prince's "Had U," or an easy-to-digest Pointer Sisters ballad with a song from Eugene McDaniels's *Headless Heroes of the Apocalypse*. Just like you want some food to stand out, even if it's not for everyone, you want some songs to pop.

Figure out multiple speakers.
I don't know your audio setup. I'm not going to meddle. Maybe you have a sophisticated Sonos network that extends throughout your house. But maybe you're just streaming music from your phone to a Bluetooth speaker. In that event, I am going to recommend that you do a little research to find a way to stream to multiple speakers simultaneously. You don't want all your guests clustered in the same corner where they can hear the music. But you also don't want too much different music playing in different parts of the party. People should be hearing the same thing. It helps with a sense of oneness. (Exceptions include the bathroom, where you can always have softer jazz or R&B.) Bluetooth speakers are pretty cheap these days, and there are apps that let you play the same song simultaneously on multiple devices.

Discourage too much technology on the part of your guests.
This is a good general rule. Try to put your phone away, and ask your guests to do the same. But there's a specific dimension when it comes to music. You don't want your guests to hear a song that inspires them and immediately Shazam it, or to ask you who's singing and go on Spotify to save songs for later. Those are for later. A party is for communal experience. Questions and conversations about music can be encouraged, but they should happen between humans.

Don't come up short.
You don't know how long your dinner party will last. You might think two hours and it goes until 4 A.M. Just as this book includes late-night snacks for when things get going again, make sure you have an extra hour of music for the late night stragglers. If you start with noise, don't let things fall into silence. It will feel jarring.

INDEX

A

Afrika Bambaataa, 152, 211
Afro-Caribbean cooking, 123
aioli, *96*, 97–98
Air-Fried Chicken Burgers, 132, *133*
Akwid, 73, 209
The Album About Nothing, 104
Ansel, Dominique, 12, 211
appetizers, 47
    Chickpeas and Spinach Tapas, 48,
        49
    Crab Rangoon, *50*, 51
    New Orleans–Style BBQ Shrimp
        and Burrata Toast, *60*, 61–62
    Perfect No-Roll Crab Roll, *52*, 53–
        54
    Poached Chicken Wraps, 55–56, *57*
    Sweet Potato Kimchi Pancake, *58*,
        59
Armisen, Fred, 35, 209
Arnold, Dave, 184, 211
Arrington, Nyesha, 59, 209
arrival music, 213
Ask Rufus, 145
Audio Two, 82, 209
Avalon, Frankie, 175
avocado, *40*, 41

B

Bacharach, Burt, 165
bagna cauda, 88, *89*
Bailey, Mashama, 152, 211
Baker, Chet, 55
Balboa, Rocky, 175
Baldino, Joey, 175, 211
basil, 88, *89*
basmati rice, 116–17, *118–19*. *See also*
    rice
"Batterram" (Tee), 59, 209
Baxtrom, Greg, 51, 209
BBQ Sauce, *60*, 61–62
Beach Boys, 103, 210
beans

Chickpeas and Spinach Tapas, 48,
    49
    Chocolate Chili, *66*, 67
Beastie Boys, 184, 211
the Beatles, 53
Becerra, Camille, 55–56, 209
Le Bernardin, 25
Biel, Jessica, 165, 211
Big Night, 192
Birbiglia, Mike, 206
Biscuit Crackers, *26*, 27
"Black Beatles" (Sremmurd), 88, 210
"Blame It on the Boogie" (Jacksons),
    121
Blistered Shishito Peppers, *44*, 45
Blueberry Crunch Cake, *164*, 165
"Blue in Green" (Davis), 55, 209
Blue Trombone, 147
Bok Choy and Cucumber Salad, *80*, 81
bologna, *190*, 191
Bomb Squad, 68
Boogie Down Productions, 35, 209
Bourbon Raspberry Tea, 180, *181*
Bowie, David, 28
Braised Osso Bucco, *154*, 155
bread
    Burrata Toast, *60*, 61–62
    Corny Shortcakes with Strawberries
        and Sour Whipped Cream, 171,
        172, 173
    Garlic Fried Breadcrumbs, 111–12
    Grape Focaccia, *36*, 37–38, *39*
    Lemon Cornbread, *96*, 97–98
    Sourdough Toast, *24*, 25
"Break It All" (Los Shakers), 53, 209
Bring It On, 180
British Invasion, 53
Brown, Ardenia, 42, 45, 209
Brown, James, 200, 211
"Bubble Butt" (Major Lazer), 200
burgers, 132, *133*
Burrata Toast, *60*, 61–62

C

cake
    Blueberry Crunch Cake, *164*, 165
    Corny Shortcakes with Strawberries
        and Sour Whipped Cream, 171,
        172, 173
    Tiramisu Tradizionale, *174*, 175
Calderone, Athena, 141–42, 210
Calloway, Cab, 18, 209
"Can It Be All So Simple (Remix)"
    (Raekwon), 157, 211
carbs, 107. *See also* bread; pasta; rice
Cardamom Dressing, 90
Casio SK-1 sampler, 82
cauliflower, 104, *105*
caviar, 200
"Cereal Killer" (Method Man and
    Redman), 90, 210
Chance the Rapper, 111
"Change the Style" (Son of Bazerk),
    68, 209
cheese
    Mac and Cheese, *194*, 195, *196*, 197
    Pimento Cheese Dip with Biscuit
        Crackers, *26*, 27
chicken
    Air-Fried Chicken Burgers, 132, *133*
    chicken wings, 134–35, *136–37*
    Country Captain Chicken, 152, *153*
    Heidi's Million Dollar Chicken,
        134–35, *136–37*
    Jerk Chicken, *122*, 123–24, *128*
    Mom's Chicken Curry, *76*, 77
    Poached Chicken Wraps, 55–56, *57*
    Spicy Sweet and Sour Chicken with
        Lemongrass, *144*, 145–46
"Chicken Grease" (D'Angelo), 97, 210
Chickpeas and Spinach Tapas, 48, *49*
chili, *66*, 67
Chili Sauce, 55, 56
chips, 42, *43*
Chocolate Chili, *66*, 67
chorizo, 73–74

chowder, *72*, 73–74
cinnamon rolls, 12
    Cinnamon Rolls with Honey Mead
        Icing, *168*, 169–70
Cinnamon Schmear, 169–70
cioppino, 70, *71*
"Climb" (Mos Def), 51, 209
Clooney, Rosemary, 192, 211
Cocktail Spread, 28, *30–31*
Coconut Jollof Rice, 125–26, *127, 129*
Cold Turkey, 27
communal experience, 17–18, 203,
    206, 215
Congo Square, 171
"Contact" (Daft Punk), 28
cooking
    Afro-Caribbean, 123
    music and, 17
    recipe testing, 16–17
corn
    Corny Shortcakes with Strawberries
        and Sour Whipped Cream, 171,
        172, 173
    Lemon Cornbread, *96*, 97–98
    Mexican Corn Chowder, *72*, 73–74
Cosby Show, 82
Country Captain Chicken, 152, *153*
couscous, 141–42, *143*
crab. *See also* fish and seafood
    Crab Rangoon, *50*, 51
    Perfect No-Roll Crab Roll, *52*, 53–
        54
crackers, *26*, 27
creative inspiration, 15–16
Creole Spice, 116–17
Croce, Jim, 175
cucumber
    Bok Choy and Cucumber Salad, *80*,
        81
    Fruit Salad with Cucumber and
        Mint, 166, *167*
Currant Couscous, 141–42, *143*
curry, *76*, 77

D

Daft Punk, 30
D'Angelo, *97*, 125, 210
David, Hal, 165
Davis, Miles, 55, 209

De La Soul, 198, 211
Deschanel, Zooey, 81, 209
desserts
    Blueberry Crunch Cake, *164*, 165
    Cinnamon Rolls with Honey Mead
        Icing, *168*, 169–70
    Corny Shortcakes with Strawberries
        and Sour Whipped Cream, 171,
        172, 173
    Fruit Salad with Cucumber and
        Mint, 166, *167*
    Tiramisu Tradizionale, *174*, 175
Destiny, 121
A Different World, 82
dinner parties, 15
DJ Kool Herc, 152
Domino, Fats, 139, 210
Donohue, Kether, 182, 211
"Do the Funky Penguin" (Thomas, R.),
    134, 210
dress code, 204
drinks, 177, 205
    Bourbon Raspberry Tea, 180, *181*
    Ginger Beer, *178*, 179
    Kether's Favorite Cocktail, 182, *183*
    Red Skies at Night, 184, *185*

E

eggs
    Easy Veggie Party Quiche, *94*, 95,
        95
    Eggs in Purgatory, 192, *193*
    Nastassia's Baked Pasta Frittata,
        110, 111–12, *113*
"Egyptian Song" (Rufus), 145, 211
Ehsani, Melody, 166, 211
Electric Mud, 67
Elliott, Missy, 155, 211
Emancipation, 81
Epic Rap Battle, 77
"Es Mi Gusto" (Akwid), 73, 209
Evans, Bill, 55
"Everybody Eats When They Come to
    My House" (Calloway), 18, 209

F

Fallon, Jimmy, 11–12, 70, 132, 210
"Family Reunion" (Scott), 85, 210
"Family to Feed" (Starlito), 27, 209

The Farm Project, 81
Fennel Soffritto, *154*, 155
Fields, Kelly, 61–62, 209
first impressions, 23
Fischer, Chris, 157, 211
fish and seafood
    caviar, 200
    Coconut Jollof Rice, 125–26, *127*,
        129
    Crab Rangoon, *50*, 51
    Fresh and Smoked Salmon Rillette
        with Sourdough Toast, *24*, 25
    Herbed Shrimp Salad, *84*, 85–86,
        87
    Jalapeño Salmon Fish Skins with
        Blistered Shishito Peppers, *44*,
        45
    New Orleans–Style BBQ Shrimp
        and Burrata Toast, *60*, 61–62
    Perfect No-Roll Crab Roll, *52*, 53–
        54
    Shep's Maui Onion and Ginger
        Soup, 68, *69*
    South Philly Seafood Stew, 70, *71*
    Tuna Pasta à la Popowendy, *114*, 115
focaccia, *36*, 37–38, *39*
food salons, 15, 88, 107, 147
"For Goodness Sakes, Look at Those
    Cakes" (Brown, J.), 200, 211
Franklin, Brandon, 61
Fresh and Smoked Salmon Rillette,
    24, 25
Fried Green Tomatoes, *84*, 85–86, *87*
Fried Rabbit, *156*, 157, *158–59*
Fried Turkey, 27
frittata, *110*, 111–12, *113*
Fruit Salad with Cucumber and Mint,
    166, *167*
"Fuck the Industry" (Solange), 179, 211

G

games, 204–5
Garlic Fried Breadcrumbs, 111–12
Gavankar, Janina, *202*, 203–4
ginger
    Ginger Beer, *178*, 179
    Shep's Maui Onion and Ginger
        Soup, 68, *69*
Golden, Thelma, 179, 211

Goodie Mob, 42, 209
gooseberries, *122*, 123–24, *128*
Gordon, Shep, 68, 209
"Gossip Folks" (Elliott), 155
Gotti, Gail, 171
Graham, Ashley, 108, 210
Grape Focaccia, *36*, 37–38, *39*
Gray, Macy, 125
Grease Live, 182
The Grey, 152
Grilled Bologna Sliders, *200*, 191
Guacamole, *40*, 41
guest list, 15, 20–21

H
Hall, Carla, 27, 209
Hamilton, 11
"Ham 'N' Eggs" (A Tribe Called
    Quest), 195, 211
Hargrove, Roy, 125
Heidi's Million Dollar Chicken, 134–
    35, *136–37*
"Heimy's Happiness" Fries with
    Kewpie Mayo, Caviar, (and a
    Glass of Bubbles), 200, *201*
Hendricks, Jon, 70, 209
Herbed Shrimp Salad, *84*, 85–86, *87*
"Herbert Harper's Free Press News"
    (Waters), 67, 209
Holland, Tanya, 116–17, 210
"Home Cookin" (Lambert, Hendricks,
    & Ross), 70, 209
Honey Mead Icing, *168*, 169–70
hosting tips, 204–7
Hot Chicken, 27
hot dogs, 28
"A House Is Not a Home" (Bacharach
    and David), 165, 211
Humble the Poet, 77
"Hungry Heart" (Springsteen), 132, 210
Hurricane Katrina, 61

I
"I Am Very Very Lonely" (Chance the
    Rapper), 111
"I Build This Garden for Us" (Kravitz),
    99, 210
ice, 205
"Ice Water" (Raekwon), 111

icing, *168*, 169–70
"I'm Better" (Elliott), 155, 211
"In the Year 2525" (Zager & Evans),
    108, 210
"It May Be Winter Outside (But In My
    Heart It's Spring)" (Love
    Unlimited), 95, 210

J
Jackson, Mick, 121
Jacksons, 121
Jalapeño Salmon Fish Skins, *44*, 45
Jelly Roll Morton, 48, 209
Jerk Chicken, *122*, 123–24, *128*
Jerk Paste, 123–24
JJ's Sticky Ribs, 147–48, *149–51*
John, Elton, 28
Johnson, J. J., 147–48, 211
Johnson, J. J. (jazz trombonist), 147, 211
"Joint 2 Joint" (Prince), 81, 209
jollof rice, 121. *See also* rice
    Coconut Jollof Rice, 125–26, *127*,
        129
    Jollof Rice with Jerk Chicken and
        Marinated Gooseberries, *122*,
        123–24, *128*
Jordan, Edouardo, 85–86, 210
"Jungle" (Young Senators), 123, 210
Jxmmi, Slim, 88

K
kale
    Kale Walnut Pesto Pasta, 108, *109*
    Roasted Kale Chips, 42, *43*
Kether's Favorite Cocktail, 182, *183*
Kewpie mayonnaise, 200
Kid Ink, 191, 211
kimchi, *58*, 59
Kind of Blue, 55
Kombu Stock, 53, 54
Koslow, Jessica, 90, 210
Kravitz, Lenny, 99, 210
KRS-One, 35
Kuti, Fela, 125, 210

L
LaBeau, Rose, 171
LaBelle, Patti, 141, 210
Ladner, Mark, 111–12, 210

LaFaro, Scott, 55
Lakshmi, Padma, 48, 203, 209
Lamb (artist), 155
Lamb Chops, 141–42, *143*
Lambert, Hendricks, & Ross (jazz
    trio), 70, 209
late night snacks. *See* snacks
"Layers" (Royce da 5'9"), 41, 209
Led Zeppelin, 25
Lee, Swae, 88
Lemon Cornbread, *96*, 97–98
lemongrass, *144*, 145–46
Leon, Humberto, 115, 210
"Let's Get Down" (Tony! Toni! Toné!),
    116, 210
"Let's Go Get Em" (To Be Continued
    Brass Band), 61, 209
"Let the Four Winds Blow" (Domino),
    139, 210
"Life of Da Party" (Snoop Dog), 12, 37,
    209
lighting, 205
Lil Wayne, 111, 210
Lim, Carol, 115, 134–35, 210
Little Richard, 182, 211
Love Unlimited, 95, 210
"Lovin' You" (Wonder), 67

M
Mac and Cheese, *194*, 195, *196*, 197
Major Lazer, 200
"Mambo Italiano" (Clooney), 192, 211
Maple Chipotle Aioli, *96*, 97–98
Marie, Teena, 171, 211
Marinated Gooseberries, *122*, 123–24,
    128
*Martha and Snoop's Potluck Dinner
    Challenge*, 11
Matheson, Matty, 191, 211
Mattos, Ignacio, 53–54, 209
McCartney, Paul, 103. *See also* the
    Beatles
McGarry, Flynn, 88, 210
Meow the Jewels, 166
Method Man, 90, 210
Mexican Corn Chowder, *72*, 73–74
Milk Bar, 171
"Milk N' Honey" (Marie), 171, 211
mint

Fruit Salad with Cucumber and
Mint, 166, *167*
Mint Salsa Verde, 141–42, *143*
The Mixtape About Nothing, 104
#MixtapePotluck, 17
Mixtape Potlucks, 15–18
Momofuku, 171
Mom's Chicken Curry, *76*, 77
"Moonshadow" (LaBelle), 141, 210
Mos Def, 51, 209
mushrooms, *96*, 97–98
music. *See also specific artists; specific
songs*
arrival, 213
at Le Bernardin, 25
during cooking, 17
playlists, 16, 208–15
"Song Prompts" and, 12, 15–16, 18
speakers and, 215
using, 16
while eating, 17
Musk, Kimbal, 99–101, 210
M. Ward, 81
My Cousin Vinny, 82

N

Nastassia's Baked Pasta Frittata, *110*,
111–12, *113*
nectarines, 88, *89*
New Girl, 81
New Orleans–Style BBQ Shrimp, *60*,
61–62
New Soul Cooking (Holland), 116
Nigerian diaspora, 121
95 South, 180

O

"The Ocean" (Redman, J.), 25, 209
Ohio Players, 12, 169, 211
Old Dirty Basmati Rice, 116–17, *118–19*
Olmsted, 51
"100 Proof" (Johnson, J. J.), 147, 211
onions, 68, *69*
Only Built 4 Cuban Linx, 157
Onwuachi, Kwame, 121, 123–24, 210
Open Ceremony and Kenzo, 115
Open-Face Mushroom Sliders, *96*,
97–98
Orji, Yvonne, 121, 125–26, 210

osso bucco, *154*, 155
"Outa-Space" (Preston), 28, 209

P

pancakes, *58*, 59
"Past, Present, Future" (Pizzicato
Five), 115, 210
pasta
Kale Walnut Pesto Pasta, 108, *109*
Mac and Cheese, *194*, 195, *196*, 197
Nastassia's Baked Pasta Frittata,
110, 111–12, *113*
Tuna Pasta à la Popowendy, *114*, 115
paste, jerk, 123–24
"Pawfluffer Night" (Run the Jewels),
166, 211
"Pease Porridge" (De La Soul), 198, 211
*People's Instinctive Travels and the
Paths of Rhythm*, 198
peppers
Jalapeño Salmon Fish Skins with
Blistered Shishito Peppers, *44*,
45
Mint Salsa Verde, 141–42, *143*
Peppers à la Famiglia Tomei, 82, *83*
Red Sauce, 123–24
Smoky Red Pepper Sauce, 104, *105*
Spicy Green Sauce, 104, *105*
Spicy Sweet and Sour Chicken with
Lemongrass, *144*, 145–46
Perfect No-Roll Crab Roll, *52*, 53–54
pesto, 108, *109*
pie, spinach, *102*, 103
pigs in a blanket, 28
Pimento Cheese Dip with Biscuit
Crackers, *26*, 27
Pitch Perfect, 182
"Pizza," 198, *199*
Pizzicato Five, 115, 210
Plaintain Two Ways, *34*, 35
"Planet Rock" (Afrika Bambaataa), 152
plants, 205
playlists, 16, 208–11
tips for creating, 212–15
Poached Chicken Wraps, 55–56, *57*
Poehler, Amy, 95, 210
pork
JJ's Sticky Ribs, 147–48, *149–51*
pigs in a blanket, 28

Thịt Kho Tàu (Vietnamese Braised
Pork Belly), *138*, 139–40
Portman, Natalie, 103, 210
potatoes
"Heimy's Happiness" Fries with
Kewpie Mayo, Caviar, (and a
Glass of Bubbles), 200, *201*
Sweet Potato Kimchi Pancake, *58*,
59
Tomato/Potato Salad, 90, *91*
potlucks, 11–12
communal experience of, 17–18,
203, 206, 215
dress code for, 204
guest list for, 15, 20–21
invitation starting time, but no
ending time, 204
Mixtape, 15–18
tips for, 204–7
Preston, Billy, 28, 209
Prince, 81, 209

Q

Q-Tip, 195–97, 211
Questlove (Thompson, Ahmir Khalib),
11–12, 15–18, 209
quiche, *94*, 95, *95*
quinoa, 99, *100*, 101

R

rabbit, *156*, 157, *158–59*
Raekwon, 111, 157, 211
raspberries, 180, *181*
recipe testing, 16–17
Red, Hot, and Fela, 125
Red Hot Peppers, 48
"Red Hot Pepper Stomp" (Jelly Roll
Morton), 48, 209
Redman, 90, 210
Redman, Joshua, 25, 209
Red Sauce, 123–24
Red Skies at Night, 184, *185*
"Renegades of Funk" (Afrika
Bambaataa), 152, 211
ribs, 147–48, *149–51*
rice
Coconut Jollof Rice, 125–26, *127*,
129
jollof, 121–29

Jollof Rice with Jerk Chicken and Marinated Gooseberries, *122*, 123–24, *128*

Old Dirty Basmati Rice, 116–17, *118–19*

rinsing, 126

Spicy Sweet and Sour Chicken with Lemongrass, *144*, 145–46

rillette, *24*, 25

Ripert, Éric, 25, 209

Riperton, Minnie, 67

"Rip It Up" (Little Richard), 182, 211

Roasted Kale Chips, 42, *43*

Roasted Veggie Quinoa Bowl, 99, *100*, 101

Robbins, Missy, 155, 211

"Rocket Man" (John), 28

Rodgers, Nile, 125

the Roots, 11–12, 61, 70, 82, 104, 161

"The Roots Song That Wale Is On" (Wale), 104, 210

Rorschach tests, 214

Roscoe's, 67

Ross, Annie, 70, 209

Rotary Connection, 67

Royce da 5'9", 41, 209

Rudolph, Maya, 67, 209

Rufus, 145, 211

Run the Jewels, 166, 211

S

Sachs, Tom, 28, 209

salads. *See* sides and salads

salmon

Fresh and Smoked Salmon Rillette with Sourdough Toast, *24*, 25

Jalapeño Salmon Fish Skins with Blistered Shishito Peppers, *44*, 45

salsa, 141–42, *143*

sauces and dressings

BBQ Sauce, *60*, 61–62

Cardamom Dressing, 90

for chicken wings, 134–35

Chili Sauce, 55, 56

Jerk Paste, 123–24

Maple Chipotle Aioli, *96*, 97–98

Red Sauce, 123–24

rib sauce, 147–48

Smoky Red Pepper Sauce, 104, *105*

Spicy Green Sauce, 104, *105*

Schoolhouse Rock, 132

Scott, Jill, 85, 210

Seinfeld, Jerry, 104

Seinfeld, Jessica, 104, 210

Los Shakers, 53, 209

She & Him, 81

Shep's Maui Onion and Ginger Soup, 68, *69*

Shocklee, Hank, 68

shortcakes, 171, *172*, 173

shrimp

Herbed Shrimp Salad with Fried Green Tomatoes, *84*, 85–86, *87*

New Orleans–Style BBQ Shrimp and Burrata Toast, *60*, 61–62

sides and salads, 79

Bok Choy and Cucumber Salad, *80*, 81

Fruit Salad with Cucumber and Mint, 166, *167*

Herbed Shrimp Salad with Fried Green Tomatoes, *84*, 85–86, *87*

Peppers à la Famiglia Tomei, 82, *83*

Tomato/Potato Salad, 90, *91*

Tomato Salad with Nectarines, Basil, and Bagna Cauda, 88, *89*

Sigel, Beanie, 175, 211

Singh, Lilly, 77, 209

"6 Foot 7 Foot" (Lil Wayne), 111, 210

sliders

Grilled Bologna Sliders, *190*, 191

Open-Face Mushroom Sliders, *96*, 97–98

Slums of Beverly Hills, 82

small plates. *See* appetizers

Smart Girls at the Party, 95

Smiley Smile, 103

Smoky Red Pepper Sauce, 104, *105*

snacks, 23, 187

Eggs in Purgatory, 192, *193*

Fresh and Smoked Salmon Rillette with Sourdough Toast, *24*, 25

Grape Focaccia, *36*, 37–38, *39*

Grilled Bologna Sliders on Hawaiian Rolls, *190*, 191

Guacamole, *40*, 41

"Heimy's Happiness" Fries with

Kewpie Mayo, Caviar, (and a Glass of Bubbles), 200, *201*

Mac and Cheese, *194*, 195, *196*, 197

Pimento Cheese Dip with Biscuit Crackers, *26*, 27

Plaintain Two Ways, *34*, 35

Roasted Kale Chips, 42, *43*

Studio Standard (Cocktail Spread), 28, *30–31*

Tina's Cold "Pizza," 198, *199*

Snoop Dog, 11, 12, 37, 209

Solange, 179, 211

"Song Prompts," 12, 15–16, 18

Son of Bazerk, 68, 209

"Soul Food" (Goodie Mob), 42, 209

"Sounds of Science" (Beastie Boys), 184, 211

soups, stews, and stock, 65

Chocolate Chili, *66*, 67

Kombu Stock, 53, 54

Mexican Corn Chowder, *72*, 73–74

Mom's Chicken Curry, *76*, 77

Shep's Maui Onion and Ginger Soup, 68, *69*

South Philly Seafood Stew, 70, *71*

Sourdough Toast, *24*, 25

Sour Whipped Cream, 171, *172*, 173

South Philly Seafood Stew, 70, *71*

"Space Oddity" (Bowie), 28

"The Space Program" (A Tribe Called Quest), 28

speakers, 215

spices and seasonings

Creole Spice, 116–17

Jerk Paste, 123–24

Spicy Green Sauce, 104, *105*

Spicy Sweet and Sour Chicken with Lemongrass, *144*, 145–46

Spider-Man: Homecoming, 82

spinach

Chickpeas and Spinach Tapas, 48, *49*

Spinach Pie, *102*, 103

Springsteen, Bruce, 132, 210

Sqirl, 90

Square Roots, 99

Sremmurd, Rae, 88, 210

Starlito, 27, 209

Stax, 134

Stevens, Cat, 141

stew, 70, *71*. *See also* soups, stews, and stock

Stewart, Martha, 11–12, 37–38, 203, 209

stock, 53, 54. *See also* soups, stews, and stock

strawberries
Corny Shortcakes with Strawberries and Sour Whipped Cream, 171, *172*, 173
Fruit Salad with Cucumber and Mint, 166, *167*

Studio Museum, Harlem, 179

Studio Standard (Cocktail Spread), 28, *30–31*

Stupak, Alex, 73–74, 209

"The Style You Haven't Done Yet" (Boogie Down Productions), 35, 209

Superwoman, 77

"Superwoman (Where Were You When I Needed You)" (Wonder), 77, 209

Sweet Potato Kimchi Pancake, *58*, 59

"Sweet Sticky Thing" (Ohio Players), 12, 169, 211

T

Tag Team, 180, 211

tajadas, 35

tapas, 48, *49*

"Tattoo of My Name" (Kid Ink), 191, 211

TBC. *See* To Be Continued Brass Band

technology, 215

Tee, Toddy, 59, 209

Thịt Kho Tàu (Vietnamese Braised Pork Belly), *138*, 139–40

Thomas, Haile, 97–98, 210

Thomas, Rufus, 134, 210

Thompson, Ahmir Khalib. *See* Questlove

Tien, Kevin, 139–40, 210

Tina's Cold "Pizza," 198, *199*

Tiramisu Tradizionale, *174*, 175

toast
Burrata Toast, *60*, 61–62
Sourdough Toast, *24*, 25

To Be Continued Brass Band (TBC), 61, 209

tomatoes
Fried Green Tomatoes, *84*, 85–86, *87*
Tomato/Potato Salad, 90, *91*
Tomato Salad with Nectarines, Basil, and Bagna Cauda, 88, *89*

Tomei, Marisa, 82, 209

Tonight Show, 11–12, 132

Tony! Toni! Toné!, 116, 210

"Top Billin" (Audio Two), 82, 209

Tosi, Christina, 171–73, 211

tostones, 35

T-Pain, 77

Tramp Stamp Granny's, 182, *183*

A Tribe Called Quest, 28, 195, 198, 211

Trotter, Tariq, 70, 82, 209

Tucci, Stanley, 192, 211

Tuna Pasta à la Popowendy, *114*, 115

U

Union, Gabrielle, 180, 211

Uruguayan Invasion, 53

V

Vandross, Luther, 165, 211

veal, *154*, 155

"Vegetables" (Beach Boys), 103, 210

vegetarian dishes, 93, 125. *See also* sides and salads; snacks
Easy Veggie Party Quiche, *94*, 95, *95*
Open-Face Mushroom Sliders with Maple Chipotle Aioli, *96*, 97–98
Roasted Veggie Quinoa Bowl, 99, *100*, 101
Spinach Pie, *102*, 103
Whole Roasted Cauliflower with Two Sauces, 104, *105*

Vietnamese Braised Pork Belly, *138*, 139–40

Voodoo, 97

W

Wale, 104, 210

walnuts, 108, *109*

Wareheim, Eric, 200, 211

waste, 206

"Water No Get Enemy" (Kuti), 125, 210

Waters, Muddy, 67, 209

West Africa, 121

"Where's My Opponent" (Sigel), 175, 211

whipped cream, 171, *172*, 173

White, Barry, 95

White, Jarobi, 198, 211

Whole Roasted Cauliflower with Two Sauces, 104, *105*

"Whoomp! (There It Is)" (Tag Team), 180, 211

"Whoot, There It Is!" (95 South), 180

Wilson, Brian, 103

Wonder, Stevie, 67, 77, 82, 209

Wonder Woman, 77

"Work It" (Elliott), 155

wraps, 55–56, *57*

"WTF" (Elliott), 155

Wu-Tang Clan, 157

Y

Yellin, Dustin, 41, 209

Young Senators, 123, 210

YouTube, 77

Z

Zager & Evans, 108, 210

Zimmern, Andrew, 145–46, 211